THE
French Fry
COMPANION

THE French Fry COMPANION

A Connoisseur's Guide
to the Food We Love

DAVID GRAULICH

LEBHAR-FRIEDMAN BOOKS
NEW YORK

LEBHAR-FRIEDMAN BOOKS
A company of Lebhar-Friedman Inc.
425 Park Avenue
New York, New York 10022

Library of Congress Cataloging-in-Publication data
Graulich, David J.
The French fry companion : a connoisseur's guide to the food we love / David Graulich.
p.   cm.
ISBN 0-86730-760-9 (cloth : hc.)
1. Cookery (Potatoes).   2. French fries—Anecdotes.
3. Cookery, American.   I. Title.
TX803.P8G73   1999
641.6'521—dc21   98-55743
CIP

BOOK DESIGN AND COMPOSITION BY KEVIN HANEK
SET IN ADOBE MINION

Manufactured in the United States of America on acid-free paper
99   00   01   02   10   9   8   7   6   5   4   3   2   1

To my pack:

Rebecca and Buddy

CONTENTS

CHAPTER 1 • The Fry Mystique 1

CHAPTER 2 • Fried Facts and Spud Stats 11

CHAPTER 3 • Ancestral Roots 17

CHAPTER 4 • Industrialized Fries 33

CHAPTER 5 • Fry Wars 51

CHAPTER 6 • Secrets of the Fry-Meisters 61

CHAPTER 7 • Local Legends 75

CHAPTER 8 • Frontiers of Fries 89

CHAPTER 9 • Meditations on a Fry 101

ACKNOWLEDGMENTS 111

PHOTO CREDITS 113

INDEX 115

THE
French Fry
COMPANION

Chapter One

THE FRENCH FRY MYSTIQUE

T HERE HAVE BEEN some remarkable number-two acts in the 20th century—supporting players who have skillfully, unselfishly, and gracefully assisted a bigger star's rise to prominence. Sammy Sosa helped propel Mark McGwire to a home run record. Smokey Robinson had the Miracles. Dean Martin stayed in the background as an affable crooner, while Jerry Lewis clowned his way to stardom.

Then there is the french fry, the most lucrative and popular supporting player in all of food.

While hamburgers have achieved corporate, culinary, and cultural superstardom, the fry is a faithful and indispensable side dish. Hamburgers and french fries rank number one and number two as the most frequent items on American menus, according to the National Restaurant Association. One-quarter of all meals served in American restaurants come with fries. The casual query at the cash register, "You want fries with that?" has become a stock phrase and punch line.

When we are children, french fries are the first grown-up food—

The classic, straight-cut french fry is as unassuming as it is irresistible

Ray Kroc, first CEO of McDonald's

tillery of the empire is the french fry. "A competitor could buy the same kind of hamburger we did, and we wouldn't have anything extra to show," confided the late Ray Kroc, the former chief executive officer of McDonald's. "But french fries gave us an identity and exclusiveness because you couldn't buy french fries anywhere to compete with ours."

usually lathered in ketchup—that our small fingers can handle. It's one of the first foods that we share with our parents. When we are adults, french fries are the second-most popular food that we eat when drunk; number one is pizza. Whether consumed in an elegant restaurant, a fast-food site, or in the home, french fries are the closest thing we have to a universal food.

McDonald's is known as a hamburger chain, but the real heavy ar-

The star of the McDonald's empire

Since McDonald's and Burger King are the two most heavily advertised brands in the United States—not just among food brands, but of *all* brands—it isn't exaggerating to say that these marketing empires are built on a foundation of french fries. When Burger King took direct aim at the McDonald's fry with its "Stealth Fries" campaign in 1997, it triggered a marketing war whose repercussions are still being felt in the fast-food industry.

Unlike the hamburger, the pizza slice, or the hot dog, french fries are team players. No one eats a single fry. Instead, fries work anonymously and collectively as accompanists to whatever protein is featured at the center of the plate. Fries stoically endure a topping of ketchup, vinegar, gravy, mayonnaise, salsa, green chile, or melted Cheez Whiz with quiet resilience.

It's not just a burger thing. Any world-class rack of sauce-smothered hickory-smoked beef ribs should appear at the table with an entourage consisting of a tub of coleslaw, an ice-cold beverage, and a huge, steaming mountain of fries. Furthermore, french fries are one of the few foods that are consumed during each phase of the day: breakfast, lunch, dinner, between-meal, and late-night snacks.

"I don't think there is any food in this country more popular than french fries," said the late James Beard in his book, *James Beard's Simple Foods*. "Children scream for

> *Unlike the hamburger, the pizza slice, or the hot dog, french fries are team players. No one eats a single fry.*

them and adults are equally addicted." Food writer Brad A. Johnson adds: "It's hard to imagine a world without french fries. Life would be less enjoyable, surely. Dusted with salt and always eaten while still too hot, fries are one of life's most decadent pleasures." Television personality Joan Lunden says, "Show me a person who doesn't like french fries and we'll swap lies."

Calvin Trillin, the *New Yorker* essayist who has written extensively on food, says, "People are always coming around to talk french fries with me." Chef Marta Sgubin writes in her book *Cooking for Madam: Recipes and Reminiscences from the Home of Jacqueline Kennedy Onassis*: "I have my own special way of making french fries. They come out soft and nice in the middle and with a great crunchy crust. I made them for the kids all the time, and Madam loved them too."

French fries have subtle, overlooked benefits. Dr. Ray Sehelian, a Los Angeles-based sleep specialist, says that eating french fries before bedtime can help overcome jet lag and induce relaxation; it has to do with their high carbohydrate level. Fries even provide perspective on a hectic career, as actress Cameron Diaz told *Details* magazine: "I really have a great time acting. You can eat french fries day in and day out, but every once in a while, you get one that is really satisfying." Best-selling romance novelist Nora Roberts has one of her impassioned characters declare: "Barb, how can one live without french fries. Not well, I say. In fact I've been known to say a day without fries is like a day without an orgasm."

Cocktail Nation, the nickname given to the hip after-hours scene in urban America, loves the fry. "It's 2:30 in the morning," writes Maya Kukes, entertainment writer for Portland's *Oregonian*, "and as great as that last-call snakebite will go down, you're convinced that french fries would truly make the moment. Not just any soggy-drive-up-win-

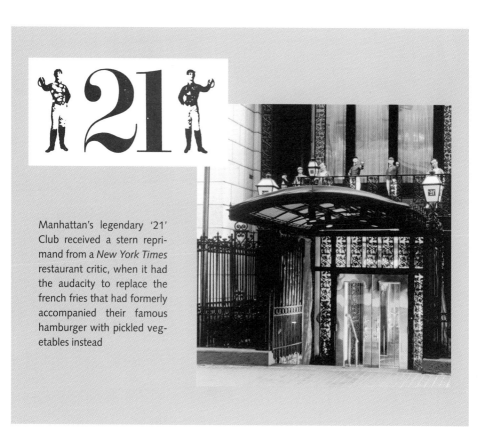

Manhattan's legendary '21' Club received a stern reprimand from a *New York Times* restaurant critic, when it had the audacity to replace the french fries that had formerly accompanied their famous hamburger with pickled vegetables instead

dow kind of fry, mind you. You're talking grease-drenched morsels that flirt with crispiness, alongside a perfect little pool of ketchup."

In the 1988 movie *A Fish Called Wanda,* french fries were the comic means by which the villain, played by Kevin Kline, extracted information from a lovable dolt, played by Michael Palin. Roger Ebert praised *Wanda*'s french fry scene as having "a nice sort of fish-and-chips symmetry."

In the hands of a master story-

The charmingly named Suzy Q's are a popular spiral variety

teller, french fries can shine, albeit in their traditional role as low-key supporting player. Consider the understated yet gripping performance by french fries and how crucial a role they played in relation to the taut feeling of suspense in this excerpt from Jonathan Kellerman's 1997 thriller, *Survival of the Fittest.* An L.A. police officer has just entered a Hollywood coffee shop:

Open twenty-four hours a day, Go-Ji's welcomed them all. The coffee shop sat on the north side of Hollywood Boulevard, east of Vine, between a tattoo parlor and a thrash-metal bar...The cop's stare bothered Terrell. Hoping it was someone else under scrutiny, he looked across the aisle at the three transsexuals giggling and whispering and making a big deal out of eating french fries.

Food critics unleash their furies if a restaurant botches the fries. Ruth Reichl, writing in *The New York Times*, reprimanded Manhattan's legendary '21' Club: "The famous hamburger, good as it is, now comes with pickled vegetables instead of french fries. Please!" Another *Times* restaurant critic, Fran Schumer, scolded a new microbrewery in Princeton, New Jersey: "That the menu doesn't have character isn't tragic. That the french fries are soggy, is."

Nutritionists and health authorities, who usually take a hard-line stance against fast food, extend an olive branch of dietary tolerance to fries. "If watching your fat grams means banishing french fries from your diet, don't despair—our tempting oven-baked version fills the void quite nicely," says Kathy Farrell-Kingsley, food editor of *Vegetarian Times*. British writer Colin Tudge, in his book *Future Food: Politics, Philosophy and Recipes for the 21st Century,* ration-

alized a low-fat recipe for fries with this statement:

I am insulting you with this simple recipe just to make a few generalizations. French fries are food for kings and [are] far from unacceptable nutritionally.... Their chief drawback is their tastiness. They encourage greed.

This book is an appreciation of the most sensational supporting act in all gastronomy: the french fry. Far more than a snack, french fries are a triumph of U.S. business and a sterling example of the American knack for converting a European custom into something distinct, populist, and, above all, profit-making. While we offer a respectful nod of recognition to those amiable fried-potato inhabitants of the breakfast and luncheon platter—hash browns, home browns, potatoes O'Brian, side o' browns, and *latkes* (potato pancakes)—they are not french fries. To paraphrase a famous Supreme Court ruling, you know a french fry when you see one.

Befitting a multibillion-dollar industry, an abundant and bewildering patois of trade jargon prevails. French fries enter the processing plant as mere spuds and go out into the dining world as spirals, cross trax, lattice cuts, steak fries, Crispy QQQs and crispy cubes, shoestrings, Skincredibles, Mega-Crunch Juliennes, Krunchie Wedges, Rough Out Thin Cuts, Junior JoJo's, Suzy Q's, and my personal favorite, the much-revered and highly esteemed Colossal Crinkle Cuts. The french fry fraternity is diverse, noble, and kaleidoscopic.

We will stroll through the food labs, Idaho farms, executive suites, restaurant kitchens, and other strategic locations throughout the domain of the fry. There will be cameo appearances by Spanish conquistadors, Thomas Jefferson, and Marie Antoinette. We'll meet John Richard Simplot, an American original whose personality is a blend of John Wayne, Li'l Abner, and J.R. Ewing from *Dallas*. We'll encounter an industrial engineer whose ingenuity brought the world the french fry scoop.

We'll click on a french fry Web page described as "an international shrine built with love and ketchup." We'll learn about a partnership between songwriter Isaac Hayes, best known for his *Shaft* music, and Mr. Potato Head. We'll meet a struggling Pennsylvania company trying to introduce a french fry vending machine. We'll learn the secrets of the fry-meisters for cooking memorable, crisp, delicious french fries at home without burning down the house.

Let the frying begin.

From Crinkle Cuts to Crispy QQQs, the fry universe includes a myriad of shapes, sizes, and textures

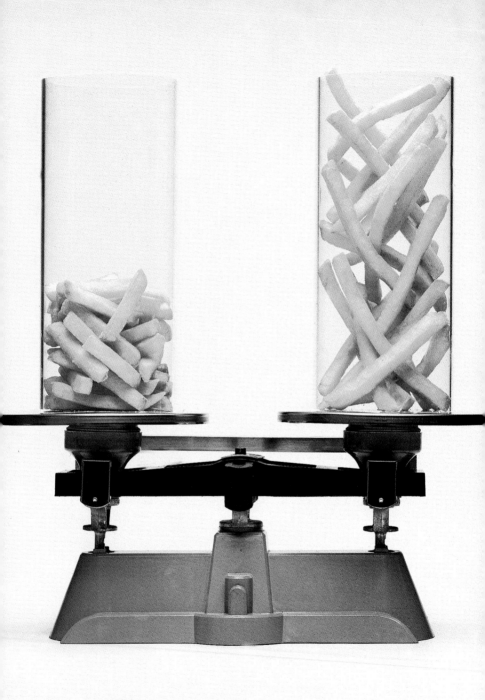

Chapter Two

FRIED FACTS AND SPUD STATS

RENCH FRIES SEEM most comfortable when they're paired with large numbers. Combine their popularity, pervasiveness in the food-service industry, overseas consumption, and huge volume, and the result is mind-stretching numbers usually associated with NASA scientists or congressional economists.

A good place to start the numerical tour is money. French fries are the most profitable food item in the restaurant industry. The more you eat, the more money the restaurant makes.

According to one french fry manufacturer: "As serving sizes increase, food costs go up very little, but profits rise dramatically." That's why restaurants are eager to have you order a "super-sized" side of fries.

Here are other fried facts and spud stats:

One out of every three potatoes grown in the United States is sliced into french fries.

McDonald's uses 7 percent of potatoes harvested in the United States, or 2.4 billion pounds. That's more than one-third of all fries sold in the food-service industry.

Laboratory science continues its relentless quest for the perfect french fry

Fry Facts at a Glance...

- About 75 percent of fast-food customers eat their french fries in a car, office, or home, rather than in the restaurant.

- Prior to the frozen-fry era, McDonald's used a specially made shortening known as Formula 47, which was a blend of vegetable oil and refined beef fat. The name came from the price—47 cents— of a McDonald's meal at that time: a 15-cent hamburger, 12-cent fries, and a 20-cent milk shake.

- Potatoes are grown in 77 percent of the world's independent countries. An acre of potatoes yields almost as much food as two acres of grain.

- Among the alternatives to potatoes that are used for french fries are yucca—a starchy root— parsnip, and rutabaga.

- The ideal frying time is between three and four minutes.

Burger King uses more than 700 million pounds of fries annually. The chain estimates that it sells 1.7 billion units of french fries each year.

Each outlet of Jack in the Box, whose fry selection includes "Chili Cheese Curly Fries," sells at least 2,000 orders of fries per week.

Every second of every day, McDonald's serves approximately 136 4-ounce portions of french fries.

Some restaurants will fan out french fries over a dinner plate so that they take up a lot of space. This is done to create the perception of oversized, generous portions.

According to the U.S. Department of Agriculture, Americans

consume more than 131 pounds of potatoes per capita each year. Of that total, about 40 percent of the consumption, or around 52 pounds, are french fries.

French fries are the most popular way that Americans eat potatoes, followed by mashed and baked, in that order.

The latest scientific trend involves fry-coating technologies. "Coated fries" are being developed on the theory that coatings reduce the amount of oil absorbed into the potatoes when fried—thus making the fries more healthful to eat. Some coatings are made from potato or wheat starch, others from a compound called pectin.

Laid end-to-end, McDonald's serves enough french fries in the United States every year to circle the equator 497 times.

The average length of a McDonald's fry is 3 inches.

A medium order of shoestring fries, the long, skinny kind, would measure around 8 feet if each fry

were laid end-to-end. It is recommended that you order about 2 feet of fries for every foot that you are

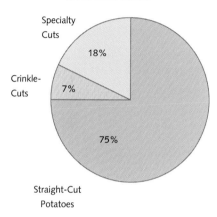

FRENCH FRIED POTATO CUTS
(% MARKET SHARE)

Specialty Cuts — 18%
Crinkle-Cuts — 7%
Straight-Cut Potatoes — 75%

tall. For example, a youngster who is 4 feet tall would enjoy a medium order.

Straight-cut potatoes—the kind most fast-food restaurants serve—hold a commanding 75 percent share of the fry market, followed by crinkle-cuts with 7 percent. Specialty cuts, such as waffle and wedge fries hold the rest of the market.

Skin-on frozen fries have failed

in the fast-food business; customers seem to think that the fries are dirty or defective. However, skin-on fries are popular in steak houses, where diners associate the skin with a fresher, higher-quality fry.

Exports of french fries rose from $1.7 billion in wholesale sales during 1989 to $2.5 billion in 1997. Exports of frozen fries now account for about 9 percent of U.S. potato production.

In Asia, Japan consumes about one-half of fry exports, followed by South Korea, Hong Kong, Taiwan, and the Philippines.

One out of every three potatoes grown in the United States is sliced into french fries.

Economists have noted a statistical correlation between the emergence of a country's middle class and increased consumption of french fries. Many economists theorize that, as a country starts to industrialize, one of the first things people start buying with their new disposable income is a serving of french fries.

It takes about 3 pounds of raw potatoes to produce 1.5 pounds of frozen french fries.

When making french fries at home, figure on using one good-sized potato per person.

Chapter Three

ANCESTRAL ROOTS

Let the sky rain potatoes.

― WILLIAM SHAKESPEARE, *THE MERRY WIVES OF WINDSOR*

THE POTATO HAS BEEN the subject of monumental scholarly research. Those books trace the potato's panoramic history through centuries of invasions, migrations, famines, revolutions, and enlightenments. "This is the vegetable that conquered the world: the peasant's staff of life, the gourmand's delight, nutritious, delicious, lauded, and maligned—the paradoxical potato, the amazing spud," proclaimed anthropologist Richard E. Rhoades in a 1982 *National Geographic* article, "The Incredible Potato."

It would be nice to report that the french fry played a prominent role throughout this epic drama, but that is not the case. It makes fleeting appearances here and there, but it wasn't until the late 20th century that the fry became a significant force in the tuber universe.

However, the early potato chronicles do have tantalizing hints about the fry of the future. The potato's origins are in the high, arid plains of Peru, where Andean tribes cultivated more than 100 varieties of the plant that still are raised in current times. These hardy potatoes can

Russet Burbanks, the industry standard
for slicing into french fries

The potato was an important staple of the ancient tribes of Central and South America

survive the thin atmosphere, radical temperature swings, severe frosts, and nutrient-poor soils. Most of the Andean potatoes wouldn't look familiar to a North American—some resemble miniature pineapples; others look like bright, red cherries or purple gumdrops.

Among the more exotic potatoes that remain household standards in Peru are the *mishipasinghan*—"nose of the cat," which the tuber supposedly resembles—and an especially knobby, difficult-to-cook, and frustrating variety called *lumchipamundana*, "potato that makes young bride weep."

The Quechua Indians, who predated the Incas, developed a food called *chuño* that is still a staple. *Chuño* is essentially a freeze-dried potato that is prepared by alternating cycles of freezing and drying. Richard Rhoades, the anthropologist, described the process as follows:

> When the heaviest frost falls in the Andes, small bitter potatoes are spread on the ground for exposure to the night's cold, and then left to dry in the sun. After several days, villagers gather them into small piles and do a rhythmic potato stomp with their bare feet. The trampling sloughs off the skins and squeezes out the remaining water. The potatoes are soaked in water for one to three weeks to reduce bitterness, and then redried. The Indians use *chuño* in soups, stews, and a sweet dessert called *mazamorra*.

Chuño also was placed in the tombs of the dead for munching purposes on their journey to the afterworld, a gesture that was surely a foreshadowing of the french fry's popularity with commuters.

Larry Zuckerman, in his 1998 book *The Potato: How the Humble Spud Rescued the Western World,*

draws a parallel: "Today we think of fast-food potatoes as french fries, but *chuño*, whose recipe is several thousand years old, softened rapidly in boiling water and was quickly ready to eat."

While hauling back gold and silver to Spain, the conquistadors tossed a few potato plants on their galleons as curiosities. They even may have practiced the rhythmic potato stomp during idle hours. Pedro de Cieza, a member of Francisco Pizarro's expedition, praised potatoes in 1539 and described them as resembling chestnuts.

In Europe, however, the potato met with what analysts today would describe as consumer resistance. The vegetable generated fear and controversy because of a case of mistaken identity. Since the mature potato plant resembles two other plants, nightshade and mandrake, which have hallucinogenic and narcotic effects, the European peasantry associated the potato with satanic powers. The intellectual classes, meanwhile, had a snobbier attitude, viewing the potato "as undignified food, fit only for beasts or people who lived like them," according to Zuckerman.

The word *potato* itself was a tongue-twisted adaptation by the English of *batata,* the term used by Arawak tribes in the Caribbean for sweet potatoes, which aren't really potatoes at all but a vine from a different botanical family. While the Andean potato languished in disrepute, the "Spanish sweet potato" surged in popularity, partly because of its pleasing, dessertlike taste and partly because it was believed to be an aphrodisiac. Indeed, England's King Henry VIII was particularly fond of them.

The man credited with bringing the potato in from the cold was an 18th-century French pharmacist and agronomist named Antoine Augustin Parmentier. His devotion to potatoes resulted from his having to survive on them during the Seven Years' War between France

and Prussia, when he set a world's record for wartime futility by being taken prisoner five times. Among his other accomplishments were getting Marie Antoinette to wear potato flowers in her hair as an ornament and convincing her husband, Louis XVI, to sport a potato flower in his lapel. If only he had persuaded her to say, "Let them eat fries," a great deal of bloodshed might have been averted.

Parmentier displayed a keen sense of showmanship that shrewd french fry marketers would adapt in the 20th century. To prove that potatoes could grow in terrible soil, he planted them on 50 acres of sandy wasteland on the outskirts of Paris. As the plants blossomed, he posted armed guards around the crops— but only during the daytime, knowing full well that peasants would sneak in during the night and steal the potatoes for consumption.

For his tireless promotional efforts on behalf of the potato some two centuries before the advent of

Henry VIII was fond of sweet potatoes, which were believed to be an aphrodisiac

Marie Antoinette wore a potato flower in her hair as an ornament,
while her husband, Louis XVI, sported a potato flower in his lapel.

the Idaho Potato Commission, Parmentier is remembered in recipes such as *crêpes Parmentier.* He also is memorialized by a statue in a Paris metro station, in which he is depicted in knee breeches and powdered wig, holding a basket of potatoes and offering a spud in an outstretched hand.

Potato cultivation and popularity spread under Napoleon, and the plant gained acceptance across Europe. The French called the potato *pomme de terre,* or "apple of the earth." In Ireland it became a di-

Under Napoleon's rule the *pomme de terre* gained in popularity across Europe.

etary staple, leading to a rapid increase in that country's population. The potato blight and famine, caused by a fungus in 1845, took a horrific toll and led to massive Irish immigration into the United States.

There also was a conflict waged in 1778-79 known as *Kartoffel Krieg,* or the Potato War. An account of that confrontation appears in a landmark work published in 1949 by the late British physician Redcliffe N. Salaman. His magnificent book, *The History and Social Influence of the*

Potato, still is regarded with awe throughout the spud community. According to Dr. Salaman, the Prussian army, led by Frederick the Great, and the Austrian army, under the generalship of Prince Henry, faced each other in a grim stalemate across the River Elbe in Bohemia. The opposing armies ate up all of the potatoes along the battle lines until the onset of winter and then called off the fighting. "The part played by the potato was essentially a passive one," Dr. Salaman concluded.

Dr. Salaman's contributions to the advancement of the potato were so extraordinary—he passed away in 1955 at the age of 81—that his career deserves recognition by french fry devotees. An eminent pathologist at a London hospital, he was forced by illness into early retirement in 1903, and he resided quietly and morosely in the country village of Barley. "Having no liking for golf, tennis, or cricket, I was at loose ends... None of the hobbies of my boyhood any

longer made an appeal," he wrote in the preface to his book.

Fate intervened in 1906, by way of a chance remark by Dr. Salaman's opinionated gardener, Evan Jones, who claimed to know more about potatoes than any other man living. Jones's boast aroused Dr. Salaman's competitive spirit from its torpor. Dr. Salaman began to study potatoes, first as a hobbyist and then as a zealot. Recalling his epiphany four decades later, he wrote:

Whether it was mere luck, or whether the potato and I were destined for life partnership, I do not know, but from that moment my course was set, and I became ever more involved in problems associated directly or indirectly with a plant with which I then had no particular affinity, gustatory or romantic... I embarked on an enterprise which, after 40 years, leaves more questions unsolved than were at that time were thought to exist... There have not been wanting those who have regarded these activities with a shake of the head and an indulgent smile, indicating that nothing, short of mental instability, could excuse a lifelong attachment to the study of so banal a subject.

The frying of potatoes didn't really take off until the mid-1880s, thanks to the availability of new, inexpensive fuels and cooking fats, such as cottonseed oil. Deep-fried slices of potatoes, called chips, became a popular food among the British working class, especially in seaports. James Trager, in his authoritative book *The Food Chronology*, records the opening of the first London fish-and-chips shop by a man named Joseph Malines in

Harry Ramsden founded his original fish and chips hut at Guiseley, West Yorkshire, in 1928. The Harry Ramsden's chain remains popular in England, where it serves fried fish and potatoes in the 19th-century tradition.

1864. Those shops served North Sea fish, such as cod and hake, along with deep-fried potatoes, all doused with vinegar and served in wrapped-up newspapers. Hustling workers in British port cities took enthusiastically to fish and chips.

Fish-and-chip shops acquired a reputation as malodorous hangouts for rowdy youths, a problem that Ray Kroc still would be wrestling with a century later when he sought to expand the McDonald's empire.

Fish-and-chip shops would sell their treats wrapped up in newsprint until 1968, when the British Ministry of Health outlawed the practice as nonhygienic. Some shopkeepers resorted to putting the fish and chips in plain, white wrappers and then inserting the whole greasy ensemble inside a newspaper. Despite the ministry's ruling, Britain's National Union of Journalists continued sending an annual greeting to the Federation of Fish Friers: "Your trade is wrapped up in ours."

Meanwhile, back in France, another frying approach was being utilized. "*Pommes frites,* what Americans call french fries, appeared on city streets around 1870, and the oil that fried them usually came from horseflesh, meat the lower classes ate," writes Larry Zuckerman in his *Humble Spud* book.

Immigrants brought the potato back to the Western Hemisphere, although they left behind the snobbery and superstition that had haunted the potato in the Old World. One legend attributes the introduction of the french fry to Thomas Jefferson, who supposedly brought back the delicacy after en-

Fish-and-chip shops acquired a reputation as malodorous hangouts for rowdy youths.

Legend attributes the introduction of the french fry in America to Thomas Jefferson, who reportedly brought back the delicacy after enjoying it as a diplomat in the French court

joying it as a diplomat in the French court. This is a charming story and has indisputable historical symmetry, since it implies that Jefferson not only negotiated the Louisiana Purchase and dispatched Lewis and Clark to explore it but also introduced the hot side dish that would feed the terri-tory's millions of new inhabi-tants. Regrettably, nothing in Jefferson's documents—nor anywhere else—authenticates the legend. Perhaps DNA tests ultimately will determine the truth about Jefferson's french fry paternity.

John Mariani, an American food historian, argues that the "french" in french fries doesn't refer to a connection with France. Instead, he says, the adjective referred to the method of preparation, since to "french" a food meant to cut it into thin strips. (The word *spud,* incidentally, is derived from the spade, or three-pronged digging fork, used in Ireland to raise the potato crop).

The best evidence of the french fry's existence in mid-19th-century America occurred in 1853. A chef in Saratoga Springs, New York, named George Crum was running the kitchen at Moon's Lake House resort. Crum, who was either extremely sensitive to criticism or possessed of a sardonic sense of humor, took umbrage when a patron sent back a serving of french fries, complaining that they were cut too thick. Crum responded by shaving some potatoes paper thin, frying them in deep fat, salting them heavily, and sending them back. To Crum's surprise—and the immense relief of the waiter—the patron declared himself delighted with the new dish and ordered more. Crum's "potato chips" were such a hit that he quit Moon's and opened a competing restaurant across the lake, where he perfected a dish called canvasback duck and, presumably, adapted more conventional customer service techniques.

"French fries and potato chips are essentially the same entity, differing only in shape and thickness," says Lee Edwards Benning in *The Cook's Tales: Origins of Famous Foods and Recipes*. "What Americans call a french fry, the English call a chip, and the French call *pomme de terre paille* (julienned and of the very narrow, matchstick size), *pommes frites chip, en liards* (thin crisp, or *pomme Pont-Neuf* (thick-cut)."

With the inherent American trait for tinkering, the potato underwent various genetic alterations on its journey to fast-food eminence. Rev. Chauncey E. Goodrich of Utica, New York, bred a lineage from South American seedlings that he dubbed "Garnet Chile," which other breeders used as stock for a potato called "Early Rose." Almost every potato in the United States can trace its lineage back to those two tuber patriarchs.

In 1872 the American horticulturist Luther Burbank used an Early Rose in his New England garden to develop an elongated white tuber known as the Russet Burbank, or Idaho potato. Together with its tastiness and adaptability to different cooking methods, the long shape made the Russet ideal for slicing into french fries. The Russet Burbank is the industry standard and what most Americans think of when they visualize a potato. Burbank eventually moved to California, where his name now graces a Los Angeles suburb.

Luther Burbank and the world-famous Russet Burbank—or Idaho potato—which he developed. One of his rewards was to have a Los Angeles suburb named after him.

In 1876 a European visitor noted that fine American hotels offered five kinds of potatoes for breakfast—boiled, baked, stewed, Lyonnaise, and fried—and that potatoes also were served on his transAtlantic ship. "This was clear proof," says Larry Zuckerman in his potato history book, "that the homely, humble tuber could grace anyone's plate anytime without evoking the class consciousness that surrounded the vegetable in Europe. In America the potato had found a socially comfortable home."

American troops returning from Europe after World War I spoke fondly of the fried potatoes they had eaten in France and Belgium. The crunchy, hot vegetable was soon being paired with the hamburger at roadside stands across the country. However, making the fry was a labor-intensive, time-consuming, and unpleasant process, and storage of potatoes and oils was expensive and fraught with hazards. Attempts to sell a tempting frozen french fry were unsuccessful; in 1946 the New York department store Macy's briefly offered a frozen fry, and a Long Island, New York, firm called Maxson Food Systems failed in its frozen-fry attempts.

It would take the prosperity of post-World War II America, the growth of suburbs and franchising, and two outsized entrepreneurial personalities to jump-start the industrial era of the french fry.

Chapter Four

INDUSTRIALIZED FRIES

HE DEAL WAS DONE with a handshake after a day of schmoozing and horseback riding on a spacious ranch near Santa Barbara, California. The two deal-makers had much in common. Both were self-made entrepreneurs who didn't have college degrees or Establishment connections, but who combined extraordinary vision with the resolve and nerves of professional gamblers. Both were in the latter years of middle age. Both had built careers and companies by proving the experts wrong in the unglam-orous sectors of the food business.

The two men were Ray Kroc and Jack Simplot, and the year was 1967. Many years after their handshake, Timothy Egan in *The New York Times* described that fateful day in Southern California:

The king of fast-food hamburgers and the patriarch of potatoes came together for a meeting that would change the American meal and create a new breed of corporate farmer... Kroc and Simplot forged a deal to make the perfect french fried potatoes—upright, bright, cheap,

Innovation and entrepreneurship have transformed the frozen french fry into a global multi-billion dollar industry

and free of molds. They would look the same whether they were sold on the Jersey shore or in a drive-through in Idaho.

Simplot told a reporter from *Nation's Restaurant News* in 1997 that the agreement was struck along these lines:

—KROC: Okay, Jack, build me a plant, and I'll put these stores on just as fast as you can deliver them.
—SIMPLOT: By golly, boy. Let's get going.

"On the basis of that handshake of burgers and fries," said author George Gilder in his book, *Recapturing the Spirit of Enterprise*, "Simplot rushed home and launched a facility in Heyburn, Idaho, that could produce 30,000 pounds of fries an hour."

The Kroc-Simplot handshake marked the beginning of the industrialized fries epoch. Up to that point french fries were a popular

food that had to be stored laboriously, cooked, and served on-the-spot by employees with limited training. Quality varied wildly, from crisp, golden, savory fries to soggy, rectangular, yellow mush. Frozen french fries were still a theoretical dream. McDonald's was so disappointed with the taste, appearance, and texture of frozen fries that its senior executives recoiled in horror at the thought of messing around with their most profitable product.

Food writer Brad A. Johnson describes the antediluvian, everything-from-scratch era, when some 140 local grocers made deliveries to individual McDonald's restaurants:

Back then, McDonald's restaurants bought Russet potatoes in 100-pound sacks and fed them to bulky, low-tech machines that continuously peeled and sliced the tubers. Fry cooks blanched the potatoes in hot fat, then finished them in small batches as they were needed. Aside from the use of automated peelers,

Ray Kroc (far left) and Jack Simplot tour a new processing plant. The Kroc-Simplot pact marked the beginning of the industrialized fries epoch.

Ray Kroc in front of an early McDonald's restaurant. Because of him, the world would never look at the french fry the same way again.

this wasn't a revolutionary cooking process, but rather a good idea borrowed from European street-vendors, transformed into an American restaurant phenomenon.

After McDonald's went public in 1965, Kroc was worried about fries. Inability to mass produce a quality fry—one that could match the consistency of McDonald's hamburger—would be the major impediment to the rapid growth needed to keep Wall Street happy.

That was the impetus for a fried version of the Manhattan Project to find an edible, dependable, economical frozen fry (Ironically, there would be an odd overlap with the real Manhattan Project, as we'll see later). As journalist John F. Love commented in his book, *McDonald's: Behind the Arches:* "McDonald's began researching potato frying the way pharmaceutical companies research new drugs... What at first appeared to be a simple task soon seemed akin to unlocking the secrets of the atom."

McDonald's researchers wrestled with technical problems that resulted, in John Love's words, from "the fundamental aversion potatoes have to being frozen." The temperature settings on fryers didn't accurately depict the real temperature of frying oils in the vats. When a cold mass of potatoes was dropped into the oil, the temperatures would decline sharply. Some fryers would recover more quickly than others; the temperature would reset at different levels

McDonald's began researching potato frying the way pharmaceutical companies research new drugs...

Jack Simplot, young and old: a blend of shrewd businessman and gutsy gambler. His mode of operation was to go into debt, gamble on an unproved product, create it in volume, drive down costs, and wait for demand to follow.

in different fryers. Ice crystals formed inside the potatoes during the freezing process, making the fries soggy, damp, and greasy-looking when cooked.

Into that dilemma strode J.R. Simplot. The son of Idaho farmers, he started making money from unconventional ideas at the age of 14. His mode of operation was to go into debt, gamble on an unproved product that big competitors wouldn't touch, create it in volume, drive down unit costs, and then wait for the demand to follow. Simplot believed that supply would create its own demand.

That ethereal voice in the movie *Field of Dreams*—"Build it and they will come"—was describing Simplot's business philosophy as he jumped from scrap metal to onions to hogs to land to potatoes. "I ain't no economist," Simplot told an employee, "but I got eyes to see."

During World War II Simplot built the world's largest potato dehydration plant to feed American troops. George Gilder described the wartime effort made by Simplot's enterprises:

To get more spuds, he bought and cleared several new potato farms. To get more shipping boxes, he bought lumber mills and built box factories. To dispose of endless potato skins and eyes and sprouts, he built a feedlot for some 3,500 hogs. To get fertilizer for soil wilted by too many potato crops, he bought mineral rights on 2,500 acres of phosphate-rich territory.

After the war, Simplot received the Army-Navy "E" medal, given for excellent industrial performance during the war. A tribute was extended by Col. Paul Logan, the officer responsible for food procurement:

Simplot was asked to build a huge plant for which there was no precedent and when little construction material was available; he was asked to equip the plant with machinery that didn't exist and for which there was no blueprint; and to undertake a food processing procedure on which there was very little technical knowledge... Working day and night, for most of the war, Simplot and colleagues converted 600,000 pounds of raw potatoes daily into good quality condensed, and extremely useful, battlefield food product.

Potato consumption declined during the 1950s, and Simplot sought ways to expand volume. He had one unsuccessful go-around with McDonald's, when he put $400,000 of his own money into an experimental cold-storage system for Russet potatoes. The system failed, and the potatoes rotted, but McDonald's was impressed by his gamble.

Based on the handshake with Kroc, Simplot anted up $3.5 million to build a plant for the breakthrough frozen french fry process—which had yet to be discovered. Years after the deal Simplot reminisced: "I figured, hell, if the old man [Kroc] didn't take these fries, I would expand the plant for myself. It gave me a good excuse to build the kind of frozen french fries plant I wanted."

The gamble paid off. Researchers at McDonald's and Simplot discovered a process that eliminated the destructive effects of freezing by drying the prefrozen fry with air, and then putting it through a rapid frying cycle before freezing. The principle that evolved was simple: Do less cooking in the store and more cooking during production. The new process reduced the moisture while retaining the crispness of the fry.

Thus began the explosive growth of the frozen fry. By 1972 McDonald's had converted completely to

THE FRENCH FRY COMPANION

frozen potatoes, and had broken away from the rest of the fast-food industry. The fry volume became so immense that Simplot couldn't handle it all. Today Simplot provides about one-half of McDonald's fries. Several large companies compete with Simplot in the frozen fry business, such as Ore-Ida, McCain, Nestlé, and Lamb Weston. F. Gilbert Lamb, a founder of Lamb Weston, invented the formidable Lamb Water Gun Knife, a high-pressure system that hurls potatoes at a speed of 117 feet per second through sharpened steel blades, converting the whole potato into sliced french fries with astonishing efficiency.

Now, about that odd coincidence with the *real* Manhattan Project,

By 1972 McDonald's had converted completely to frozen potatoes and had broken away from the rest of the fast-food industry.

which built the atomic bomb. Most of the frozen french fry industry is located around the Columbia River Basin of Idaho, Oregon, and Washington state. This part of the Northwest isn't the green, rainy, lush region associated with Seattle, but a high, arid, windswept desert.

"More than 50 years ago," writes Timothy Egan in *The New York Times*, "President Franklin D. Roosevelt envisioned the Columbia Basin as a haven for Dust Bowl refugees who could farm the desert with the help of irrigation water provided by Federal dams and reservoirs." Huge projects such as the Grand Coulee Dam created inexpensive hydroelectricity and irrigation water.

Combined with the dry volcanic

The unlikeliest of combinations—potatoes and plutonium. General Leslie Groves headed the Manhattan Project, where his plutonium production facility shared the area with potato cultivation.

soil, the cheap energy created prime conditions for potato cultivation—and when the frozen french fry boomed in the 1960s and 1970s, the region boomed, too. During the 1940s the area was so desolate that Gen. Leslie Groves, head of the Manhattan Project, built a plutonium production facility at Hanford in southeastern Washington, figuring that if the nuclear reactor exploded, civilian casualties would be light and the atom bomb would be kept secret.

As for Jack Simplot, he went on to grow Simplot into a diversified agricultural company. He also made

another fortune in high technology by putting up $1 million in seed money for Micron Technology, a semiconductor company. At the age of 89, he still can be seen discussing crop prices and weather conditions with his friends at Elmer's Pancake House in Boise, Idaho. You may see his car in Elmer's parking lot—it's the Lincoln Continental with the license plate "MR SPUD."

❋

McDonald's french fry research yielded another important result— an object that was unglamorous, even banal, but that undoubtedly will fascinate anthropologists in the 22nd century. That object is the french fry scoop, invented by a McDonald's lab engineer named Ralph Weimer. Restaurant workers complained that the kitchen tongs used to put fries in a bag were clumsy to handle and resulted in wasted product falling to the floor. A few lost fries per bag may not sound like much, but when multiplied by hundreds of thousands of servings, the

The frozen fry, once an industry pariah, now dominates the french fry market. It takes about 3 pounds of raw potatoes to produce 1.5 pounds of frozen french fries.

economic consequences were huge. Weimer devised a V-shaped aluminum scoop with a funnel at the end that transported the fries from cooker to bag in one motion, with the fries neatly in the same vertical direction. Weimer's scoop is now standard equipment in fast-food restaurants everywhere.

Today the french fry industry is innovating busily on several fronts. As consumers become more health conscious—or at least are talking about health more—widespread attempts are being made to reduce the fat content of fries. Everyone, from giant producers like Simplot to a little Kansas City, Missouri, company called Marvel LLC, seeks market share for low-fat or fat-free fries. So far the reaction of most customers could be summarized as, "Thanks, but I'll stick with my old-fashioned high-calorie oil-laden fries." When it comes to their beloved french fries, Americans talk skinny—but eat fat.

Lamb Weston is taking a different angle by emphasizing speed.

Having diagnosed a malady called "french fry frustration," the company is appealing to fast-food operators whose customers must wait impatiently while the fries cook.

Lamb Weston's Generation 7 fries can slash cooking times by up to 50 percent or more, says the company in its advertising, staking a claim for Generation 7 as the "fastest fries in food service." The new fries also are described with a distinctive word—*ovenable*—meaning that they can be cooked in an oven rather than in a fryer.

The name of the new Lamb Weston fries—Generation 7—has a certain biblical resonance, a rhythmic cadence that connotes evolutionary transformation, and it has is a distinguished pedigree. First there was:

Generation One: The Frozen Fry, who begat

Generation Two: The Skin-on Fry, who begat

Generation Three: The Specialty Cut Fry (Curly QQQs and CrissCuts), who begat

Generation Four: The Coated Fry, who begat

Generation Five: The LW Private Reserve Process, who begat

Generation Six: The Clear Coat Fry (a.k.a. Stealth Fry), who begat

Generation Seven: The World's Fastest Ovenable Fry.

New products such as Generation 7 reflect the fry industry's attempts to sustain the sales growth that began in the late 1980s. That upswing resulted from the push toward "value meals" in the fast-food industry. The value strategy, which bundled such items as fries and a soft drink with the main item, encouraged "super-sizing," or requesting a larger order of fries than otherwise might have been purchased. The first company to emphasize the value strategy, starting around 1988, was Taco Bell. Ironically, it didn't sell french fries. However, it slashed prices on its tacos and burritos and bundled them into value meals, with chips and a soft drink, in an effort to move the company out of the Mex-

ican segment and into the fast-food mainstream.

Taco Bell made such rapid gains that other fast-food companies soon were imitating the bundling approach. "The Value Meal was a way of packaging the french fries along with the entrée in order to encourage higher volume, and it pretty much pervaded the fast-food industry," says Bruce Huffaker, editor of *North American Potato Mar-*

ket News, a newsletter in Idaho Falls, Idaho. "The years between 1988 and 1995 saw the strongest growth in domestic consumption of the french fry."

FROM FIELD TO FORK

French fry producers are always looking at ways to improve the entire system that brings the fried potato to the consumer—or, as the saying goes, "from field to fork." It starts with the variety of potato that is cultivated, stored, and processed.

"There are many technical challenges inherent in growing a potato suitable for the french fry industry," explains Dennis Corsini, Ph.D., a researcher at the USDA Small Grains and Potato Germplasm Center in Aberdeen, Idaho. "One of the biggest problems is storability. The french fry industry in the United States and Canada depends

on stored raw product to keep the plants running almost year round. Shutting down for long periods is inefficient, and the name of the game is efficiency.

"A percent or two better recovery per ton of raw product being processed makes a lot of difference in profit," Corsini continues. "That's why the new varieties, such as Ranger Russet, are a big improvement over the old industry standard Russet Burbank. However, when you look at the storability of the crop as a whole, Russet Burbank is still the best variety for storage periods of eight months or more. It doesn't dehydrate as readily, nor rot as easily, as other varieties that are suitable for large-scale frozen french fry production. Russet Burbank can be held at intermediate temperatures (45–47°F or 7°C) for 8 to 10 months without accumulating unacceptable sugar levels. It has relatively long dormancy, so it is easily sprout-inhibited compared with most other varieties."

Regrettably, even the mighty Russet Burbank has vulnerabilities, Corsini says. "It is very susceptible to stresses and most field diseases. It is a battle for farmers and fieldmen to meet the demands of the french fry production plant. The production people want uniformly sized tubers, with a high proportion of large tubers for the premium cuts; uniformly good solids—the 21- to 23-percent range is ideal—and lack of internal defect problems, such as hollow heart, internal brown spot, internal blackspot, stem end discoloration, sugar end, and net necrosis, which are all defect problems that Russet Burbank is quite susceptible to, along with a susceptibility to diseases such as Verticillium wilt, early blight, late blight, and leafroll.

As consumers become more health conscious— or at least are talking about health more— widespread attempts are being made to reduce the fat content of fries.

"We have overcome many of these problems with some of the new varieties, but I don't see Russet Burbank being replaced yet for long term storage. At least one variety (we have proposed the name Gem

Russet) can probably be held as long as Russet Burbank with minimum problems.

"The grower must produce a potato crop of uniformly high internal quality (high solids, low sugars, minimum defects) that will store well for many months. This requires high fertilizer and pesticide inputs to keep diseases, insects, and weeds to a minimum. But the grower of Russet Burbank is still at the mercy of Mother Nature, who can cause a number of problems," Corsini says.

Asked whether he envisions genetic engineering of bionic fries, Corsini replies: "New varieties developed by traditional breeding programs, such as ours, will continue to steadily replace some of the Russet Burbank acreage. Genetically engineering the Russet Burbank may help to alleviate some of the disease problems but is unlikely to solve the whole complex of environmentally related stress reactions that are typical of the variety. I believe this would require extensive changes in the physiological makeup of the variety, and we don't have the knowledge to do that now. By the time we do have the knowledge and technical capability, Russet Burbank already may be replaced for a good share of the frozen french fry industry."

Chapter Five

FRY WARS

Try the fry, America!

— FROM A BURGER KING ADVERTISEMENT

THE FRENCH FRY world's version of a mega-confrontation—its Ali-Frazier heavyweight title fight, its dream altercation—began in 1997, when Burger King challenged the fry supremacy of the reigning champ, McDonald's, with a $70 million marketing campaign to tout its "hotter, crispier, and tastier french fries."

Like that other epic marketing slugfest, the Cola Wars, the Fry Wars have both sides engaging in perpetual claims of victory. In August 1998 Jack Greenberg, chief ex-ecutive officer of McDonald's, declared to the *Wall Street Journal:* "The french fry war is over. We won. We make the world's best." A Burger King spokesman retorted: "It's not important what Jack says. It's important what consumers say, and they have told us they significantly prefer the new Burger King french fry."

The reformulated Burger King fry—code-named "The Stealth Fry" and coated with a batter made from secret ingredients—was backed by hype and hoopla reminiscent of a political campaign. The company

World supremacy in the battle of the fries—
this is the prize to the victor in the fry wars

obtained the rights from the Hasbro toy company to use the figure Mr. Potato Head as "official spokesspud" for the promotional campaign, which it dubbed "Decisions '98: Try the Fry, America." A claymation figure of Mr. Potato Head—similar to the famed dancing California raisins—rolled into action. A campaign biography of Mr. Potato Head noted that he was born on May 1, 1952, in Pawtucket, R.I., that he was married to Mrs. Potato Head, and that the couple had 12 small fries.

To provide musical accompaniment, Burger King signed up singer and composer Isaac Hayes to adapt his theme music from the movie *Shaft* for the new fries. January 2, 1998, was Free FryDay, and anyone entering a Burger King restaurant received a free small order of fries.

"We had a fry team comprised of about 100 people whose mission, if they chose to accept it, was to find a better fry. We think they've done it," a Burger King spokeswoman told the *Denver Post*.

> *"The french fry war is over. We won. We make the world's best."*
>
> – JACK GREENBERG,
> MCDONALD´S CEO

For Burger King, the fry wars are nothing short of a chance at redemption. The company has long been a runner-up to McDonald's for leadership in the hamburger industry. Founded in the 1950s by the late James W. McLamore and David R. Edgerton, Jr., Burger King began as a small Florida chain. The development of a jumbo-sized broiled burger—The Whopper—transformed Burger King from a regional competitor into a national one. "Our idea of the great American meal was a Whopper, fries, and a Coke, and we sold that idea," McLamore said in his autobiography, *The Burger King.*

Then came a series of missteps that threw Burger King off-stride just as McDonald's— aided by its stunning conversion to frozen fries—was gaining momentum.

One mistake was an attempt, in the early 1990s, to diversify away from the fundamental pairing of burger and fries. This was the "dinner basket" strategy, in which customers could order a steak sandwich, fried (frozen or breaded) shrimp, or a breaded thin chicken cutlet, served in a basket. After ordering at the counter, the basket would be brought to their table by Burger King personnel. While they waited for their meals, diners could munch on free popcorn.

As McLamore scathingly described in his memoirs, the dinner basket strategy and expanded menu were calamities:

The most popular dinner basket turned out to be a Whopper with french fries, which shouldn't have surprised anyone because these two items were long established as the most popular items on our regular menu. There was nothing new about this. Our customers were trying to tell us that they wanted a Whopper and fries and were not particularly inter-

> *"It's not important what Jack says. It's important what consumers say, and they have told us they significantly prefer the new Burger King french fry."*
>
> – A BURGER KING SPOKESMAN

ested in marginal-quality dinner items that we were ill-equipped to properly prepare and serve anyway. The dinner-basket concept was never thoroughly test-marketed, but I am certain that our franchisees would have killed the idea if they had been given a voice in the matter. Even in the face of evidence that our restaurants were selling less than 20 dinner baskets a day, we kept the program alive for almost a year and a half. It was reported that we spent over $40 million trying to promote this idea.

Learning from its mistakes, Burger King decided that it already held a slight advantage over McDonald's in burgers. So triumph in the burger war really came down to who had the better fries.

So who has really won the fry wars? Actually, both McDonald's and Burger King are winners, because they elevated the question of who has the better fries into a national—and international—debate. *French Fry Companion* conducted its own taste test, as will be described in a later chapter. We also dropped into a Web site devoted to opinions on french fries (Cybersight's Original French Fry Survey, www.lincolnnet.net). Some comments from the fry files:

The challenger for the Fry Wars title and some of its tools of battle

The defending champion and one of its high-energy television ad campaigns

BK's new fries are now my favorite! They always seem to be hot when I buy them and they are crunchier and more potatoey tasting than McD's fries.

– *Theresa, Englewood, Md.*

McDonald's, because they are so light and crispy.
– *Russell, Canberra, Australia*

Burger King—hot, crispy, taste good.

– *Robert, Uniontown, Pa.*

McDonald's fries are the all-time best. I love them. I eat them at least three times a week because they are the greatest.

– *Michelle, Palm Bay, Fla.*

I like the new Burger King fries but I still like McDonald's too.

– *Keisha, Chicago, Ill.*

Fries at McDonald's can be great sometimes, or they can be really soggy.

It is potluck. However, the *old* Burger King fries were always crispy and the champs. The new Burger King fries are really bad.

– *Matt, Cincinnati, Ohio*

McDonald's

®

McDonald's fries are the best ever. They have a grate [sic] taste and are a cool golden color. They are also gust [sic] the right size.

– *William, New Brunswick, Canada*

We like any kind of french fries, as long as they're hot, crispy, and a little salty, like the ones Mom and Dad make! Yum! They taste so-o-o-o good. We love them (the french fries and Mom & Dad).

– *Adam, Shalom, Josh, and Shawna, Shirley, Ark.*

Miami-based Burger King got an unexpected local recommendation when a 13-year-old multitransplant patient named Daniel Canal left the University of Miami's Jackson Children's Hospital after receiving three sets of four transplanted organs. The teenager's first solid food after his surgical ordeal was an order of chicken tenders and french fries from Burger King. His assessment of the fries: "Actually, I think they were a little bit better than I remembered."

James W. McLamore (right), co-founder of the Burger King chain, pictured in front of an early Burger King unit in Florida, virtually unchanged from its original appearance (top)

✣ *Chapter Six* ✣

SECRETS OF THE FRY-MEISTERS

NE OF THE CHARMS OF the french fry is that you can enjoy it at home as well as in a restaurant. The frozen variety is prepared easily in the oven, stove, or microwave. If you are a little more ambitious and remember to buy a sack of potatoes at the grocery store, you can explore the culinary delights of making your own fresh french fries.

Many variables go into achieving the quintessential fry: choice of potato, heat of oil, length of time, and whether you choose a one- or two-step process. Here are some insights, tips, opinions, and general fry wisdom from the high priests of the french fry domain:

Marta Sgubin, chef and author
Cooking for Madam: Recipes & Reminiscences from the Home of Jacqueline Kennedy Onassis

"I use small red potatoes and cut off the round edges so they are little blocks, then I quarter them so they are small cubes. I cook them in hot Mazola or canola oil, of course, fresh each time. I heat the oil, then drop the potatoes into it and cover

If you are a little more ambitious and remember to buy a sack of potatoes, you can explore the culinary delights of making your own fresh french fries

61

Chef Marta Sgubin writes in her book *Cooking for Madam: Recipes and Reminiscences from the Home of Jacqueline Kennedy Onassis:*

"I have my own special way of making french fries. They come out soft and nice in the middle and with a great crunchy crust. I made them for the kids all the time, and Madam loved them too."

the pan for two or three minutes. It's sort of like parboiling. But if they stay covered too long, they disintegrate, so they should just sort of steam.

"Then I remove the lid and continue to cook until the potatoes get nice and brown. When they are done, I spread them on a jelly roll pan lined with paper towels so the fat is taken away. Then I salt them and serve them immediately."

**Bill and Cheryl Alters Jamison,
authors**

Born to Grill

The Jamisons recommend rubbing the potato slices with spices to promote crusting. Their All-'Round Rub is a blend of paprika, black pepper, kosher salt, chili powder, brown sugar, and cayenne. Grill the potato spears over medium-low heat for 30 to 35 minutes, turning them every five to 10 minutes and dabbing them lightly with oil once or twice. Cook until the exteriors are brown and crisp and interiors are soft and tender.

"These grilled fries disappear as quickly as the country ham at a Southern boarding house," the Jamisons say.

Idaho Potato Commission
How to Fry Perfect Idaho Potatoes

A handy one-page flyer from this potato trade group has cooking tips for the food-service industry in English and Spanish as well as an enlarged photograph of a chunky french fry shaded in five tones of brown, from light to dark. "Choose your ideal finished frying color," the flyer advises.

Frying the Perfect Potato…

The following guidelines come from the Idaho Potato Commission's flyer, *How to Fry Perfect Idaho Potatoes:*

- The ideal frying temperature is 350 degrees Fahrenheit.

- Blanch fresh fries to decrease fry time, control color, reduce oil uptake, inactivate enzymes, and improve texture.

- Store potatoes for fresh cut fries at 55 degrees. Potatoes stored at 40 degrees or lower will fry up too brown on the outside and be undercooked inside because of excess sugars.

- Use 10-ounce potatoes, or larger, to produce better length fries.

- Use number-1 potatoes for high yield. Number-2 potatoes are an economical choice that taste the same, but the yield is lower.

Michel A. Mes

The Belgian Fries Page

www.belgianfries.com

This Web site argues that what Americans call french fries really

political party in Flanders, as he eats Belgian fries from a *frietzak,* or paper wrapper. The Web site offers these tips:

- Start by peeling some potatoes.

- Do not slice them too thin. One

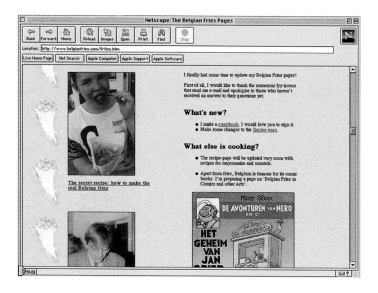

should be appreciated as Belgian fries. Fans of obscure Benelux politicians will appreciate a grainy photograph of Guy Verhofstad, former chairman of the third-largest

centimeter square is the perfect dimension. Try to cut them rectangular; pointed ends tend to burn.

- Do not put too many fries into

the fryer at once. The oil will cool down, and your fries will be too wacky and greasy.

- Do not fry them the first time until they become brown.

- Never put a lid on your frying pan. This makes your fries wacky.

- Heat to 190 degrees Centigrade (375 degrees Fahrenheit) and fry for two minutes until the fries are crispy and golden brown. This way they will be crispy on the outside and soft on the inside, the way they *should* be!

The Official French Fries Page

www.tx7.com/fries

This Web site is a compendium of history, opinion, and trivia, con-structed by an irreverent bunch of fry enthusiasts. The *Washington Post* described the site as "an international shrine built with love and ketchup." Among its treasures, visitors will find nine pages of U.S. Federal Code that regulate the production and sale of french fries, art work such as "Hindu Ketchup," and a list of 22 things to do with french fries besides eat them (Number 12: If you are trying to quit smoking, a french fry has a similar size and shape and can be held in the hand just like a cigarette. Number 16: When the batteries in the remote control are dead, a well-thrown french fry can change the channel.)

> *"If you are trying to quit smoking, a french fry has a similar size and shape and can be held in the hand just like a cigarette."*
>
> – THINGS TO DO WITH FRENCH FRIES BESIDES EAT THEM

French Fry Love

Finalist, First Tri-Annual Blue Mountain Arts
Poetry Card Contest, 1997

A father,
And his little boy
Eating lunch
At a drugstore
Where I was sitting,
Waiting for hamburger to go.

Were talking.
Little boy talked most.
Words muffled through french fries
And came out,
"Ah vluvoo"
And continued to chew.

Alice B. Toklas
The Alice B. Toklas Cook Book (1954)

This classic volume, written during an era that was much less fat-phobic than today, enthusiastically described "The Real Right Way for French Fried Potatoes:"

Peel the potatoes, cut them all of the same size and length. Put them in moderately hot oil, lard or very white beef fat—there should be enough so that the potatoes are not crowded. When the potatoes come to the surface, remove them from the fat at once. Let the fat reheat quickly, increase to highest flame. The potatoes should not be out of the fat more than two minutes. Plunge them into the fat for the second time and remove at once. Sprinkle with salt and serve at once.

Chris Thayer's Baked French Fries
14-year-old student,
Rye Middle School, Rye, New York

The teenager's recipe appeared in the magazine *Vegetarian Times.* Two medium baking potatoes are cut into quarter-inch slices and baked for 20 minutes in a preheated 425-degree oven. The recipe wins the effusive praise of Kathy Farrell-Kingsley, *Vegetarian Times's* food editor: "Oven-baking results in a crispy, golden exterior and tender, moist interior that's irresistible. Plus, these fries are a cinch to make and our technique works wonder- fully well with other tubers or root vegetables, such as carrots, sweet potatoes, and parsnips."

James Beard

James Beard's Simple Foods

The late master chef had a great deal to say about frying potatoes. One of his more intriguing tips could be characterized as the "health spa" ap- proach to making fries:

Place the prepared potatoes in cold or ice water and let them rest for several hours. Then remove them and dry thoroughly. I find that a large bath towel is the best thing for drying. Spread out the towel, lay the potatoes on it, and roll it up until the water is absorbed.

Beard devoted a chapter to frying techniques for various dishes in his book and had additional recom- mendations specifically for french fries:

The potatoes can be fried at once in deep hot fat (375 degrees F), lower- ing a few at a time in the basket. Do not overcrowd or the temperature of the fat will drop, and the potatoes will be soggy and greasy instead of crisp. Let them cook until they are a deep golden color. They will turn themselves in the bubbling fat. Once they are cooked they should be placed on absorbent paper. Check the temperature of the fat between fryings. If you are cooking a large quantity of potatoes, put each batch in a 250 degree F oven to keep warm until all of them are done.

There is another style of fried potatoes that I am fond of these days, and it requires shredding. I put mine through the shredding attachment of the Cuisinart food processor. These little strings of potatoes need only be lowered into hot fat for a few seconds to become delicately crisp and lovely in flavor. They can be served in a great bird's nest of a mound on a heated dish or used as a garnish for a roast.

Steve Holzinger, chef and columnist
www.globalgourmet.com

Holzinger provides a useful glossary for the different cuts and variations of the fry:

Allumette: Cut into matchstick shapes, about 2-3 inches long.

Shoestring: Like Allumette but longer, 3-5 inches, and about an eighth-inch in diameter.

Julienne: Somewhere between Allumette and Shoestring, but thicker, perhaps ¼ inch.

Pont Neuf: Should be a half-inch in diameter, at least 5 to 6 inches long.

Soufflé: Very mature potatoes are peeled, cut in half on the long axis, and cut in half-circles one-eighth-inch thick. They are rested in ice water for a half hour and blanched soft at 300 degrees F. They are finished in 400 degrees to puff and served in a boat-folded linen napkin.

What's in a Fry?

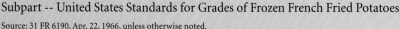

Government bureaucracy even extends to the french fry. Following, the legal definition of a french fry, according to government standards:

Subpart -- United States Standards for Grades of Frozen French Fried Potatoes

Source: 31 FR 6190, Apr. 22, 1966, unless otherwise noted.
Redesignated at 42 FR 32514, June 27, 1977 and at 46 FR 63203, Dec. 31, 1961.

52.2391 PRODUCT DESCRIPTION

Frozen french fried potatoes are prepared from mature, sound, white or Irish potatoes (Solanum tuberosum). The potatoes are washed, sorted, and trimmed as necessary to assure a clean and wholesome product. The potatoes may or may not be cut into pieces. The potatoes are processed in accordance with good commercial practice which includes deep frying or blanching in a suitable fat or oil and which may include the addition of any ingredient permissable under the Federal Food, Drug, and Cosmetic Act. The prepared product is frozen and stored at temperatures necessary for its preservation.

Dean Fearing, chef

The Mansion on Turtle Creek
Dallas, Texas

The recipe for "Dean's Favorite French Fries" appears in a sumptuous book, *Burger Meisters: America's Best Chefs Give Their Recipes for America's Best Burgers, Plus the Fixin's*. Chef Fearing's fries are seasoned with a mixture of cayenne pepper, fresh sage, thyme, and ground white pepper, and fried in vegetable oil at 360 degrees until golden brown and crisp. He suggests using six large Idaho potatoes for four servings, although the chef cautions: "This recipe is proportioned for spud lovers. If your appetite is not Texan in nature, use four Idaho spuds rather than six."

We conclude this fry-meister sampler with two anecdotes that have more to do with the masterful eating of fries, rather than their preparation.

First is the testimony of Jeffrey Steingarten, food critic for *Vogue* and author of *The Man Who Ate Everything and Other Gastronomic Feats, Disputes and Pleasurable Pursuits.* While researching a magazine story that compared ketchup brands, Steingarten and his wife developed a fry-buying strategy:

"Let the games begin," my wife said

as we walked into our neighborhood McDonald's. Next to the deep fryers is a bin where cooked potatoes languish under heat lamps until somebody orders them, by which time they may taste like cardboard. So we stood unobtrusively in the condiment and napkin area and waited and watched. When the holding bin was nearly empty and the assistant manager had dropped some fresh potatoes into the deep fryer, we rushed up to the counter and requested ten large orders of fries. A few minutes later we were walking back home with our crispy treasures.

Finally, there is this tale of celebrity french fry consumption from Mike Bayer, who runs a public relations firm in Laguna Beach, California:

I was working at Disneyland in the early 1960s at the Carnation restaurant next to the Magic Castle (I graduated to driving a submarine after that). Vincent Price, the actor, came to my window to place an order. He wanted a hamburger with everything on it, including about six or seven french fries on top of the meat. I told him we did not make them that way and he could order some fries and fix it himself.

No go. He did not want a whole order of fries, just six or seven on the hamburger. I shoved a napkin through the window and said, "Okay, sign the napkin and you got it." He did, and I got him his french fries hamburger.

Benita's
FRITES
WORLD'S
GREATEST FRIES

Chapter Seven

LOCAL LEGENDS

It's midnight… and you need fried food. Welcome to Nirvana.

— *EAT OUT* MAGAZINE REVIEW OF POMMES FRITES, NEW YORK

THE *FRENCH FRY Companion* sought local legends whose french fries are paragons of potato pulchritude. Nominations came from restaurant critics and food writers as well as from fry fanciers who responded to queries posted on Internet forums. Those people contributed a vast compendium of fry-centric experience and represented the collective wisdom of many frequent fryer miles.

We salute a few of those local legends here—restaurants both grand and humble. In doing so, we pay homage, by proxy, to the thousands of restaurants serving up great french fries in cities, hamlets, bus terminals, strip malls, country roads, and highway exit ramps all over America.

Benita's Frites

Santa Monica, California

A small place in a food mall near the beach, Benita's "tops everyone's list for best french fries," according to the *Los Angeles Times*. People tend to eat Benita's fries while they

Benita's Frites in Santa Monica, California. The *Los Angeles Times* says Benita's "tops everyone's list for best french fries."

are strolling along a promenade and observing what the *Times* calls "the

Benita's Frites
Santa Monica, California

oil—and serves them up in a paper cone with a choice of toppings and dressings. The owner, who is Belgian, named the business after his sister. During peak summer months Benita's uses more than 5,000 pounds of potatoes per week.

Luis Alvarez, manager of Benita's, says the place is popular with tourists, and he can guess a person's nation of origin based on the

changing cast of unusual characters and entertainers. A string quartet. Magicians. A man in top hat and tails doing the soft shoe on roller skates."

Benita's puts Kennebec potatoes through a two-step process—steaming, then frying in canola

topping chosen for the fries: "The American way is ketchup. People from Belgium and Holland like mayonnaise. English people like gravy. Asians and Latins like things spicy—garlic and lemon, chiles, jalapeño."

Bob's Famous Fries
Gardiner, Maine

Every summer in this small town in south-central Maine, a man named Bob parks his old, blue bus with red trim near the intersection of Water and Bridge streets. He sells bowls and plates of french fries, cooked to order, and hands them out the bus window with a folded paper towel. Bottles of white and apple vinegar are available for spritzing the fries.

Jane and Michael Stern, who write a delightful "Road Food" column for *Gourmet*, discovered Bob's Famous Fries during his months of operations—April through July only. The

Sterns described Bob's fries as "pale, thick sticks with creamy insides. You can get hamburgers and hot dogs, too, but most visit this ad hoc eatery for nothing but the potatoes."

Pat's King of Steaks
Philadelphia, Pennsylvania

Another discovery by Jane and Michael Stern, Pat's claims to be where the famed Philadelphia cheese steak was invented more than 60 years ago. This open-all-night sandwich stop serves up freshly made french fries immersed in gooey layers of melted Cheez Whiz. "The drippy molten cheese makes finger-licking an essential part of the dining experience," the Sterns report. "The best way to eat Pat's fries is standing up, elbow-to-elbow with the most discriminating of Philly chowhounds."

Peter Luger
Brooklyn, New York

This venerable steak house is over-looked by most tourists, who stay in midtown Manhattan and don't venture to the outer borough of Brooklyn to experience what former *New York Times* restaurant critic Ruth Reichl calls "the best steak in New York City."

If the steak isn't enough to justify a taxi ride over the Brooklyn Bridge, consider what Reichl says about Peter Luger's premier side dish: "The french fries have been terrific every time I've tried them. They come out hot and crisp with a powerful potato flavor; dipped into butter and beef juice in the bottom of the platter, they are absolutely wonderful."

Peter Luger
Brooklyn, New York

Pommes Frites

New York, New York

Located on Second Avenue between Seventh and Eighth streets, Pommes Frites serves Belgian-style, double-cooked fries. The magazine *Eat Out* says, "It's midnight. You're drunk, and you need fried food. Welcome to Nirvana. Pommes

Pommes Frites
New York, New York

Frites's fries are so good—hot, crispy, and salty—that this storefront need not sell anything else, save a selection of 28 mostly mayo-based toppings." Jonathan Scull, writing in *Atlantic Monthly*, chimes in: "If your stomach demands attention, hop over to Pommes Frites. Smother the Belgian fries with exotic toppings, or try the house *frite* sauce from the Netherlands. Perfection in a fry—it's to die."

Primanti's

Pittsburgh, Pennsylvania

French fries are a big attraction at this Steel City institution, which has expanded to several sites. According to Joel Kundin, a Pittsburgh attorney, "Primanti's is the most famous restaurant in Pittsburgh. It started as a sandwich shop that was open all night in the 'strip district,' where the city's produce is delivered. The drivers would go in there at all hours. Sandwiches are huge and are served in wrapping paper. Two huge hunks of fresh bread are overstuffed with meat, and the french fries are served right on the sandwich. According to local lore, the custom started so that truck drivers could eat the sandwich with one hand."

The sandwich that made Primanti's famous:
The fries are served right on the sandwich

Al Forno
Providence, Rhode Island

George Germon and Johanne Killeen, a husband-and-wife team own this award-winning, 110-seat restaurant. They cut potatoes into matchsticks and fry them only after they are ordered. "When I tasted the fries in Italy and France, I realized I had discovered something great. The fries were the thing that really popped out at me," Germon told food writer Brad Johnson. "People love them; they look great. No matter how you cut it, there's not anything like a good french fry." Al Forno alternates among Yukon golds, size-A reds, and Russets.

Bishop's
Lawrence, Massachusetts

David Shribman is Washington bureau chief for *The Boston Globe* and has won a Pulitzer Prize for his political coverage. As he travels throughout the United States reporting on elections and campaigns, he is also a fond patron and ardent chronicler of great local food.

For the high office of best french fries, Shribman casts his vote for Bishop's, a Lebanese-American restaurant owned by the Bashara family and located in downtown Lawrence. In addition to traditional Middle Eastern dishes, Bishop's serves homemade fries. "Bishop's fries are about as good as they get, and I love to order huge quantities of them," Shribman says.

Abraham Bashara, one of the owners of Bishop's, says he prefers Idaho potatoes for frying. "We'll let them settle in a storage room before we serve them, so the sugar and water levels decline. Years ago we'd fry them in pure lard; now we use vegetable oil. We peel the potatoes ourselves and fry them fresh. A few customers make a special request; they like their fries well-well done, really brown, but most people like a nice yellow look."

McClard's

Hot Springs, Arkansas

Known since 1928 for its beef and pork barbecue, McClard's also goes through about 2,000 pounds of Idaho white potatoes per week for its gargantuan side dishes of french fries.

"We buy potatoes in a 10-pound bag and put them through a hand-slicer to get half-inch wedges with about half the skin on," says John Thomason, a member of the family that owns the restaurant. "We pre-fry the potatoes in vegetable oil about halfway through for maybe a minute and then pull them. When we get an order, we put them back in and finish it. For some reason it just turns out different than if we fried them once."

The most popular dish is the "rib and fries" platter of barbecued beef with a double order of french fries. The idea is to dunk the fries in the thick barbecue sauce. If you get sauce on your fingers and face, so much the better. "People around here love barbecue sauce on their fries, although some people put ketchup and mayonnaise on them," Mr. Thomason says. The

McClard's goes through about 2,000 pounds of Idaho white potatoes per week to make its fries

recipe for the sauce is kept in a safety deposit box in a Hot Springs bank. Legend has it that a stranger stayed at the McClard family's inn during the 1920s. He was broke, and the only way he could pay was with his barbecue recipe. He left town, never to be heard from again, and the McClards went into the barbecue business.

McClard's, which seats about 90 people, is located in the outer regions of Hot Springs near the intersection of two highways. "There's not a whole lot where we are at," Mr. Thomason says.

Holman's
Portland, Oregon

Maya Kukes, entertainment writer for *The Oregonian,* recommends the fries at this "classic neighborhood bar.... cozy and dark, where the creaky old booths almost swallow you up" and relates this conversation with a friend:

"You want fries with that?"

"Have I really eaten all these fries?" my drink companion asked, her eyes wide with fear.

"She had, indeed. At Holman's the fries are that good."

Le Caprice
London, England

Our sole European local legend is recommended by R.W. "Johnny" Apple, Jr., longtime political and diplomatic correspondent for *The New York Times.* Writing in the magazine *Forbes ASAP,* Apple cited french fries as a favored dish as he named his favorite European restaurants "after 35 years of tucking in my napkin at tables all across the continent, in every country on the map except Albania (which plays in the gastronomic bush leagues, anyway), and throwing caution to the wind in countless bistros, brasseries, trattorias and temples of haute cuisine." Apple recommends Le Caprice, on Arlington Street, where "the *pommes allumettes* (skinny french fries) are knockouts."

Hildebrandt's
Williston Park, New York

Steve Rushmore is president of HVS International, a consulting firm that appraises hotel and resort properties. A constant business traveler, Steve puts together for friends and clients an informal newsletter that describes his "road food" finds in unusual locations. After one speaking appearance on hotel industry economics, he catered a get-together with food flown in from his discoveries around the country, such as Skyline Chili in Cincinnati and Maurice's Piggie Park in West Columbia, South Carolina. "It was a cocktail party combined with a road food extravaganza," he recalls.

If there's a place for french fries on Steve's road food Mount Rushmore, the honor unquestionably would go to Hildebrandt's, a 75-year-old institution on Long Island. "Remember the soda fountain/sandwich shop down on the corner where they made their own ice cream, ground their own hamburgers, and hand-cut their fries?" Rushmore asks. "Hildebrandt's still does. They make absolutely the world's best fries. While my wife, Judy, a registered dietitian, has been unable to alter my eating habits over the past 30 years, she does enjoy Hildebrandt's lemon chicken Caesar salad. I'll have the burger, fries, and coffee soda, please."

Al's Number One Italian Beef
Chicago, Illinois

Al's hand-cut french fries are recommended by Izzy Kharasch, former executive chef of Harvard University's Faculty Club and currently president of Hospitality Works, a restaurant consulting firm based in Chicago. "People in Chicago like a little thicker fry, one that's greasier and served hotter," Kharasch says. "I love the fries at Al's. There's usually a line out to the street. On Valentine's Day I have a little custom of stopping at Al's on Taylor Street and bringing home two Italian beef sandwiches, french fries, and a bottle of Dom Perignon."

order fries with toppings, uses Idaho and Washington State potatoes, and fries them in Crisco canola oil.

"Canadians understand 'fries as a meal,' while my experience with Americans is that fries are strictly a side dish," says Livie Silva, director of marketing for the company. "The one thing that constantly amazes me is the emotional attachment

New York Fries

Toronto, Canada

This Canadian chain is located primarily in shopping mall food courts. It was founded by brothers Jay and Hal Gould, who discovered a fry shop—since closed —in New York's South Street Seaport and took the concept north of the border. The company sells cooked-to-

The Canadian french fry chain with the American name: New York Fries understands the concept of 'fries as a meal'

customers have to our product. Fries are the ultimate comfort food, and they cross all age/gender/demographic boundaries."

The most popular topping is beef-based gravy. About 20 percent of orders are for a dish called *poutine*, a Quebec-born meal that is popular across Canada. The fries are served in a dish, and cheese curd is added and topped with hot gravy. "Perhaps because of our British ties, Canadians also love vinegar and lots of salt on their fries," Silva says.

As part of its tongue-in-cheek marketing campaign to emphasize its fresh fries, New York Fries created an ersatz organization called SPUDHOPE—the Society for the Preservation of Undue Degradation and Humiliation of Potatoes Everywhere. SPUDHOPE opposes what it calls "factory fries" and issues a passionate call for "the humane and ethical treatment of potatoes."

Nathan's
New York City region

Arthur Bryant Barbecue
Kansas City, Missouri

Nathan's—isn't that a hot dog chain? Yes, but no less of a food maven than Calvin Trillin, in his 1974 book *American Fried: Adventures of a Happy Eater,* was ecstatic about fries at the original Coney Island site. Trillin paid the ultimate compliment of comparing Nathan's to his dining shrine, Arthur Bryant Barbecue restaurant in Kansas City, Missouri: "I have stated in public that Arthur Bryant's is to the smooth kind of french fries what Nathan's Coney Island branch is to the fat kind with krinkly edges… The french fries at Nathan's and Bryant's are interchangeably delicious." Trillin described an interview with Murray Handwerker, president of Nathan's:

Nathan's prefers Maine potatoes…
Mr. Handwerker says Idahos are fine

for baking—the people in Idaho shouldn't be mad—but too measly for a firm french fry. Long Island potatoes have too much water in them for french fries. He says Long Island are good for chowder. I guess they float well.

"At a party one night, a respectable-looking mother of three told me that Nathan's french fries (at their original Coney Island branch, it goes without saying) are at their finest just after the corn oil is first poured into the Pitman Frialators, before 9:30 in the morning."

Trillin also told a complex story about his frenetic research on behalf of his next-door neigh-

bor and new restaurant owner, "the ferociously named Zohar Ben Dov. Anticipating Zohar's request for help, I started eating french fries all over town to refresh my palate—having left the field for a few months to look after a well-deserved case of fatness... On quiet afternoons, when my mind wanders, I still see myself as Zohar's french fry consultant."

The fries at the original Coney Island Nathan's are the pinnacle of the "fat kind with krinkly edges," according to food maven Calvin Trillin

Chapter Eight

FRONTIERS
OF FRIES

THE WORLD OF FRENCH fries is a restless landscape, perpetually seeking new directions, fresh markets, and technological innovations. Here are viewpoints on the frontiers of fries from three different perspectives: The Inventor, The Traveler, and The Visionary.

THE INVENTOR

The automated french fry machine—serving up appetizing hot fries to customers and sumptuous profit margins to investors—is the Holy Grail of the fry industry. The commercial prospects of a french fry vending unit adjoining every soda machine at every gas station —or in every college dormitory filled with students craving late-night munchies—get entrepreneurs, investment bankers, and small-cap fund managers drooling.

Regrettably, no one has managed yet to put all the pieces of a successful fry machine together. A Canadian company introduced the world's first french fry vending unit in 1975. Fumes from the hot oil belched black smoke out the rear of the ma-

French fries are emerging in new forms on every horizon—culinary, industrial, even as a symbol of affluence for the Third World's developing middle class

chine, and the business failed. Today several companies are pursuing the dream of a machine, such as potato giant Ore-Ida, a Swiss-based company called Tege; Mirco Technology of Denver, Colorado, and Tasty Fries Inc. of Blue Bell, Pennsylvania.

Edward C. Kelly is chief executive officer of Tasty Fries, whose stock (TFRY) trades publicly on the NASDAQ Bulletin Board. Kelly was running a small industrial design and engineering shop near Philadelphia when Tasty Fries' predecessor company, Adelaide Holdings, hired him as a consultant to make an engineering assessment of their fry machine, which used frozen spuds.

The automated french fry machine—serving up appetizing hot fries to customers and sumptuous profit margins to investors—is the Holy Grail of the fry industry.

"I agreed to take a look, because I figured I might be able to sell them some circuit boards," Kelly says.

His appraisal of the machine? "I told them that it was the worst thing I had ever seen in my life. It violated every engineering principle I knew. It was so bad, I told them to kick it off the side of a boat and use it as an anchor."

Nonetheless, something about the idea intrigued him. "I knew nothing about french fries," he continues. "I was a movement and materials expert." He began conceptualizing a system that, instead of heating frozen french fries, would utilize dehydrated potatoes, which would be formed robotically into fries on demand, right inside the machine.

Kelly began months of intensive research. "I became rather knowledgeable about potatoes," he recalls. While looking in the U.S. Patent Office in Washington, D.C., he discovered a patent for a dehydrated potato, issued in 1939 to the submarine division of the U.S. Navy.

"I got excited," he remembers. "This potato had a shelf life in excess of two years. Five guys held the patent. Four of them had died, but one of them was still alive. In fact, he was still working for a potato company in Idaho."

Kelly negotiated for the patent rights with the surviving patent holder and raised money to overhaul Adelaide, which was rechristened as Tasty Fries. Kelly's system works this way:

🖎 Customer deposits money (about $1 for a portion about the size of a small McDonald's fries).

🖎 Dry potato pellets are gravity-fed into a setting chamber.

🖎 Potatoes are rehydrated with warm water and formed into exactly 32 french fries.

🖎 The fries are extruded into a mini-cook pot containing pr

heated oil. The portion cooks for about 60 seconds.

✎ Hot french fries are dispensed in a cup. Salt and ketchup are attached to the bottom of the cup.

"This isn't just a vending machine; it's a food processing machine," Kelly says.

Even with the improved technology, it hasn't been an easy road for Tasty Fries. As of October 1998, the company hadn't begun mass producing its machines and accumu-

lated a deficit of $12.1 million. The stock, which traded as high as $10 a share in 1994, was priced at 49 cents a share in November 1998. Yet Kelly's enthusiasm for his rehydrated fries is undampened. "Put this machine in a college dorm, and it will sell 150 to 200 orders a day. Every gas station in the world will sell them next to the Coke machines. I never met anybody who doesn't like french fries. Our biggest problem will be building these machines fast enough."

THE TRAVELER

As the economies of Asian countries began unraveling in July 1997, after Thailand devalued its currency, Richard Read faced a dilemma. Read, the international business writer for Portland's daily newspaper, *The Oregonian*, was seeking ways to explain the complex situation. Dense academic discussions of exchange rates, central banks and currency floats would be more than most readers could wade through.

"I started thinking about how to tell the story," Read recalls. "I began thinking about what gets exported from the Pacific Northwest. Then I tried to think of something immediately identifiable to everyone and which was 'value-added'—that is, it was processed or manufactured here, as opposed to a raw commodity. I could help readers understand a very dry topic if I could come up with something like that."

Eureka—the french fry.

Read discovered that french fries were a $2 billion industry in the Northwest, including cultivation, processing, storage, and transportation. Having spent eight years as a journalist in Asia, he knew that the emerging middle class there loved American fast food. Why not use the french fry to tell the story of the Asian crisis and its impact on the U.S. economy? What if he were to follow a shipment of fries across the Pacific and report on what happened every step of the way?

Some of my editors thought the whole idea was wacky. They didn't get it. They asked, "You want to follow a french fry around the world?"

"Some of my editors thought the whole idea was wacky. They didn't get it. They asked, 'You want to follow a french fry around the world?'" Ultimately, Read got approval and began his fry journey, which would become a four-part series in October 1998, entitled, "The French Fry Connection." Kathryn Scott Osler, a staff photographer, accompanied him.

"There is something humorous about french fries, and I didn't want to make light of the very real suffering in Asia and the severity of the crisis," Read says. He wrote in the opening to the series:

Following 20 tons of potatoes halfway around the world is a whimsical pursuit. A french fry is an incidental item, a ketchup-drenched side dish in fast food's global glut. Yet fries are also a study in mass production and global competition and an uncanny barometer of economic health. The fate of one particular load of french fries, and the lives and

cultures of those who handled it, illuminates the causes and effects of Asia's anguish the way no economic treatise ever could... Because french fries targeted Asia's new middle class, and the growth of the middle class is an important measure of prosperity, fries are a surprisingly accurate yardstick of economic health.

Read began his reporting on a 20,000-acre potato farm in eastern Washington State operated by a religious group, the Hutterites. While they are similar in beliefs and appearance to the Amish, the Hutterites utilize modern technologies, such as computers and credit cards. On part of the farm, known as Circle 6, the Hutterites grow as many as 5,000 tons of potatoes, enough to make about 14 million large servings of fries. Read's story tracked one particular shipment that could make about 113,000 large McDonald's servings.

The fry trail led from the Circle 6

potatoes to a Simplot processing plant in Oregon, where the plant was inspected and approved as Halal, acceptable under Islamic law, by a Muslim cleric. The story continued on a truck that took the fries to the port of Tacoma, Washington, for shipment. Read then boarded the cargo ship *Dagmar Maersk,* whose crew consisted mainly of men from the tiny Pacific island of Kiribati.

After arriving in Hong Kong for distribution, the fry connection included riots in Jakarta, where a loyal Simplot employee risked his life to save a french fry warehouse from being torched, and the chaos leading to the resignation of President

The day Jakarta burned, Angus Karoll struggled to keep 550 tons of french fries out of the fire.

Suharto. Read also described french fry consumption in Singapore and production in mainland China.

Certain passages of Read's account sound as if they were excerpted from an international political thriller, written by a collaboration of Tom Clancy and Julia Child:

The day Jakarta burned, Angus Karoll struggled to keep 550 tons of french fries out of the fire.

Karoll, 27, a lean, wry Australian who heads potato processor J.R. Simplot Co.'s Indonesian distribution, had no time to ponder the irony of the situation. As the world's fourth most-populous country lurched toward revolution May 14th, Karoll worked to save a stash of frozen potatoes.

Karoll needed someone courageous, foolhardy or greedy enough to drive 800 gallons of gasoline through riots and fire to the french fry warehouse. The fuel would power an emergency generator to keep the spuds at 8 degrees below zero until power was restored.

Karoll found his improbable hero. He met the wide-eyed driver at the storage building and paid him generously in cash.

The potatoes were saved. But the riots took a toll far more serious than a warehouse full of french fries. More than 500 people died in Jakarta that day.

Read has heard from people who say that his narrative of a single shipment of french fries helped them understand economic concepts that they otherwise

wouldn't have attempted to grasp. "I never thought I would have found so much meaning in a french fry," he says.

THE VISIONARY

"I'm a french fry-aholic," Scott Davis says. "My wife and I always seek out the best french fries. My twin 3-year-old boys love them. I've eaten them with my parents as well as with my children. From age 3 to age 90, you are buying the same product. It sounds sort of corny, but fries are a connecting point for families—reaching into a bag of fries together, sharing together."

Davis is president of Kuczmarski & Associates, a Chicago-based management consulting firm that works with *Fortune 500* companies on building brands and market share. And he has a french fry vision. "There's an enormous opportunity for a company to become a destination point where people would go to eat french fries and take part in the total french fry experience."

Davis envisions a chain of Starbucks-type places: warm, European, nicely furnished, conducive to relaxing and socializing or reading a book. Instead of coffee, the signature product would be french fries. Instead of takeout, this fry parlor would be a place to gather and hang out.

"Right now french fries are a complementary or ancillary product that are tied to some other food. The burger wars, for example, are won at the french fry level. The idea is to shift the entire experience and the behavior pattern of consumers and say, 'Okay, french fries are at the top of the menu, and if you want to have chicken or a cheeseburger or a beverage with that, we can supply that, too. The french fry comes first and the ancillary product comes second.'"

The key is consistency, for which consumers will pay a premium, Davis believes. "The frozen french fry, eaten at home, just isn't the same experience, any more than buying the beans and making a cup of Starbucks coffee at home isn't the same as going out to a Starbucks. Going out for fries conjures up great images and emotions: the dating times in high school, married couples having a special place to go for french fries and a milk shake, licking the ketchup and salt off your fingers, families spending time together."

After years of working in food brands of all varieties, Davis believes that french fries have a date with destiny. They are a power brand of the future: "So many people love fries, from so many different age groups and walks of life. With so many loyalists out there, somebody could start a french fry revolution."

Chapter Nine

MEDITATIONS
ON A FRY

WHEN EXPERTS COMPILE lists of the most significant American innovations of the 20th century, the products they celebrate are usually from the realms of communications, medicine, and transportation: the automobile, the computer, the polio vaccine, the jet airplane. It's a good bet that none of these lists ever mentioned the french fry. Yet the french fry has impressive credentials for inclusion among extraordinary American innovations. It usually is heaped with affection, salt, and ketchup. Now it's time that the french fry received a little respect.

The french fry is a small, crunchy, edible masterpiece of product innovation. Because it is so commonplace, ubiquitous, and inexpensive, it is taken for granted—much like the zipper, the pencil, the rubber band, and the paper clip. Yet the french fry has much to teach students of innovation and entrepreneurship.

"It is absolutely essential to keep innovation simple," Peter Drucker, dean of management gurus, wrote in 1985. "Complicated innovations do not work. Effective innovations start small. They are not grandiose.

The impact of the french fry on world culture is one of the great American success stories of the 20th century

They try to do one specific thing. It may be as elementary as putting the same number of matches into a matchbox, which made possible the automatic filling of matchboxes and gave the Swedish originators of the idea a world monopoly on matches for almost half a century."

A lot of intellectual capital—to use a current business buzzword—goes into the french fry. The fry begins life as a commodity product, a potato. As any farmer will tell you, it's hard to make a living by selling a commodity. Someone always is willing to do it more cheaply, and additional capacity drives down prices.

It's when you invest intellectual capital—smarts, knowledge, savvy, gray matter—into that commodity, build value into it, and market it effectively that something magical happens. Nike does this with sneakers, Gillette with razors, Intel with computer chips, and Starbucks with a plain old cup of coffee. As Esther Dyson, economist and high-tech analyst, said in an interview with *Forbes ASAP*: "If I'm in the potato business, and prices are coming down, I've got to think about creating french fries."

Consider the experience of Izzy Kharasch, president of Hospitality Works, the Chicago consulting firm. Kharasch was working on the launch of a family-style, Texas-themed restaurant, the Alamo Grill, at the Mall of America in suburban Minneapolis. "We came up with a french fry strategy," Kharasch recalls. "We had steaks to bring in parents, but we realized that to be successful, we had to do something for kids. Kids bring the parents

Now the french fry is going global. Or, to put it more accurately, the fry is extending its international résumé.

back. So we found a machine that could cut french fries into cowboy boots and cowboy hats. We called them boots-and-hats fries. People loved them. We'd get letters from people saying, 'My kids only want to eat at Alamo Grill, because they love the boots-and-hats fries.'"

Now the french fry is going global. Or, to put it more accurately, the fry is extending its international résumé. After all, the fry is by nature cosmopolitan: it is a Yankee adaptation of a European version of a South American vegetable that is wildly popular in Asia.

In the 1998 book *Golden Arches East,* which analyzes the international expansion and cultural impact of McDonald's, Harvard professor James L. Watson explains the success of the McDonald's concept:

The keystone of this winning combination is not, as most observers might assume, the Big Mac or even the generic hamburger. It is the fries. The main course may vary widely (fish sandwiches in Hong Kong, vegetable burgers in Amsterdam), but the signature innovation of McDonald's—thin, elongated fries cut from russet potatoes—is ever-present and consumed with great gusto by Muslims, Jews, Christians, Buddhists, Hindus, vegetarians (now that vegetable oil is used), communists, Tories, marathoners, and armchair athletes. It is understandable why McDonald's has made such a fetish of its deep-fried potatoes.

In Taiwan, Watson says, french fries have become a dietary staple among young people. In China, teenagers socialize for hours over french fries, talking and flirting. In Japan, french fries helped ease a centuries-old taboo against eating while standing up. If McDonald's is the primary flagship for spreading the American way of life around the world, the engine of that flagship is, undeniably, the french fry.

Kids' Fry Taste-Testing

IT SEEMED SO EASY. Market research firms get big bucks for putting a bunch of kids around a table, feeding them french fries, and recording their preferences. Nothing to it.

In that spirit, *The French Fry Companion* invited every kid we knew and their parents to join us for a Saturday afternoon french fry taste test. A hand-picked search team fanned out over a middle-class suburban region at 11 A.M. to gather anonymously sampled fries from several of the top fast-food chains. A little after noon, the nine children, ranging in age from 3 to 12, sampled the fries one brand at a time and cleansed their palates between servings with cold water. The kids were asked to make a crayon drawing after each serving and to express their innermost emotions, preferences, and musings on fries.

Results? Inconclusive. The kids complained about all of the french fries and were merciless in their criticisms. Brand bashing was rampant. However, they also ate all of the fries with ketchup, salt, and gusto and asked for more, regardless of the brand. We did notice a follow-the-leader pattern—as soon as one youngster made a critical comment, everyone else jumped in.

Here's a sampling of the comments. *The French Fry Companion*'s main con-

clusion is vast relief that we aren't in the business of food research with children:

FAST-FOOD CHAIN NUMBER ONE
Heather: Too tough.
Steven: Stale, greasy.
Nathaniel: Can I have a pickle?
Scott: Too chewy.
Justine: Too raw.

FAST-FOOD CHAIN NUMBER TWO
Justine: There's no potato inside.
Kyle: It needs more salt.

Jackie: Raw, needs to be cooked more.
Gregory: Needs more salt.

FAST-FOOD CHAIN NUMBER THREE
Steven: Very tough, chewy, greasy.
Nathaniel: I need a pickle.
Kyle: Bad.
Fiona: I can't twist it. It's good to be able to twist it.

FAST-FOOD CHAIN NUMBER FOUR
Gregory: Soggy. Rubbery.
Stephen: Chewy, tough.
Kyle: Soggy.
Jackie: Inside too hard. It's like there's small pebbles in it.
Fiona: Mommy, I don't know how to draw a french fry.

Half
Raw
Half
over
cooked

Trash

- need
More salt / flavor

Whether in the United States or overseas, french fries ultimately conquer everything before them. Their down-to-earth appeal is irresistible. The fry future is bright. Maybe Edward Kelly of Tasty Fries will figure out how to sell a french fry vending machine. Maybe someone will come up with a low-fat fry that tastes good. Maybe I'll learn how to eat fries with melted Cheez Whiz. It has never been wise to underestimate the adroitness, adaptability, and survival instincts of the french-fried potato.

Even opponents of the fast-food industry are susceptible to the fry. Eric Schlosser, in a two-part series in *Rolling Stone* titled "Fast-Food Nation," criticized fast-food chains for eliminating small businesses, damaging the environment, selling nutritionally suspect food, and spreading uniformity. Schlosser visited a Lamb Weston french fry plant in Idaho, which he compared to an oil refinery. He was given a sample of the freshly made product at the end of his tour:

> The fries on the plate looked so familiar, yet wildly out of place in this food factory with its computer screens, digital readouts, shining steel platforms and evacuation plans in case of ammonia-gas leaks. Despite all this, the french fries were delicious—crisp and golden brown, made from potatoes that had been in the ground that morning.
>
> I finished them and asked for more.

ACKNOWLEDGMENTS

French Fry Companion is grateful to those who served as stalwart guides on our french fry expedition. We have a special debt to a few people who were particularly informative and generous with their time and knowledge. A hearty toast of gratitude—consisting of a raised, super-sized portion of golden-brown, hot, crunchy, neatly arranged french fries—to the following:

Richard Read, *The Oregonian*, Portland, Oregon

Charles Nicolas, Burger King Corporation, Miami, Florida

Dennis Corsini, USDA Agricultural Research Center, Aberdeen, Idaho

Bruce Huffaker, *North American Potato Market News*, Idaho Falls, Idaho

Steve Rushmore, HVS International, Mineola, New York

David Shribman, *The Boston Globe*, Washington, D.C.

Mark Magdaleno, Strahan Advertising, Santa Ana, Calif., and Jeff Holiway, Lamb Weston, Kennewick, Washington

Izzy Kharasch, Hospitality Works, Chicago

Scott Davis, Kuczmarski & Associates, Chicago

Barbara Pisani and Christi Nelson, Lebhar-Friedman, New York, researchers for the *Companion* series

Beth G. Klein, librarian, California Culinary Academy, San Francisco

Craig Jackson and Lucinda Walker, reference specialists, Mechanics' Institute Library, San Francisco

The children and parents who participated in our french fry tasting

Geoff Golson and Paul Frumkin at Lebhar-Friedman Books, New York, who had the original vision and enthusiasm for the *Companion* series.

PHOTO CREDITS

The Belgian Fries Page: page 65

Benita's Frites: pages 75, 76

Colorado Potato Commision: pages 46, 95

Corbis/Ali Mayer: page 22

Corbis/Bettman: pages 18, 22, 23, 27

Corbis/Gianni Dagli Orti: page 21

Corbis/Robert Maass: page 62

Dennis Gottlieb: front cover, ii

David Graulich: pages 106, 107

Harry Ramsden's: page 25

Idaho Potato Commision: pages 9, 10, 15, 16, 22, 30, 60, 64, 88

J.R. Simplot Company: pages 32, 35, 37, 43

Lamb Weston Inc.: pages vi, 6, 28, 42, 44, 45, 47, 50, 63, 92, 96, 97, 105, 109

Library of Congress/Corbis: pages 30, 68

Mansion on Turtle Creek/Dean Fearing: page 71

McCain Foods USA: pages 12, 38, 67, 70, 71, 106

McClard's: page 82

McDonald's Corporation: pages 2, 35, 56, 57, 103

Nathan's Famous: page 87

The National Archives/Corbis: page 41

Nation's Restaurant News: pages 54, 55, 59

Nestlé USA FoodServices Division: pages 99, 100

New York Fries: page 85

The Official French Fries Page: page 66

Peter Luger Steak House: page 78

PhotoDisc: page x

Pommes Frites: page 79

Primanti's: page 80

Tasty Fries Inc.: page 91

'21' Club: page 5

INDEX

Adelaide Holdings, 90–91
Alamo Grill (Minneapolis), 102–4
Al Forno (Providence, Rhode Island), 81
allumette fries, 70, 83–84
Al's Number One Italian Beef (Chicago), 84–85
Alvarez, Luis, 76–77
Andean potatoes, 17–19, 20
Arawak tribe, 20
Arthur Bryant Barbecue (Kansas City), 86
Asia, 14, 93–97, 104

baked french fries, 7, 44, 45, 68–69
baked potatoes, 13
barbecue sauce, 82–83
Bashara, Abraham, 81
batata, 20
Bayer, Mike, 72–73
Beard, James, 3–4, 69
Belgian fries, 65–66, 79
Ben Dov, Zohar, 87
Benita's Frites (Santa Monica), 74, 75–77
Benning, Lee Edwards, 29
Bishop's (Lawrence, Massachusetts), 81
blanching, 34, 64, 70, 71
Bob's Famous Fries (Gardiner, Maine), 77
Burbank, Luther, 29, 30
Burger King
    challenge to McDonald's, 3, 51–53, 54–58
    french fry volume of, 12

Canada, 47, 85–86, 89–90
Canal, Daniel, 58
cheese sauce, 12
Cheez Whiz, 3, 77, 108
chiles, 3, 77
chips, 25–26, 28–29
chuño, 18–19
Cieza, Pedro de, 19
coated fries, 3, 13, 45, 51–53, 54–58
Cocktail Nation, 4–5

Colossal Crinkle Cuts, 8
Corsini, Dennis, 47–49
cottonseed oil, 25
crinkle cuts, 8, 13
crispy cubes, 8
Crispy QQQs, 8
CrissCuts, 45
cross trax, 8
Crum, George, 28–29
cultivating potatoes, 17–29, 30, 40–41, 47–49, 94–96
Curly QQQs, 45
Cybersight's Original French Fry Survey, 54–57

Davis, Scott, 97–98
defects, potato, 48–49
dehydrated potatoes, 18–19, 38–39, 90–92
Department of Agriculture, U.S. (USDA), 12–13, 47–49
dinner basket strategy, 53–54
diseases, potato, 23, 48
Drucker, Peter, 101–2
Dyson, Esther, 102

Early Rose potato, 29
Ebert, Roger, 5
Edgerton, David R., Jr., 52
Egan, Timothy, 33–34, 40
England, 25–26, 29, 83–84
Europe, 7, 19–28, 29, 31, 81, 83–84
exports, french fry, 14, 93–97, 104

famine, potato, 23
Farrell-Kingsley, Kathy, 7, 68–69
fat-free fries, 44
fats. *see* oils and fats
Fearing, Dean, 71–72
Field of Dreams (movie), 38
fish and chips, 25–26
Fish Called Wanda, A (movie), 5
France, 20–23, 26–28, 29, 31, 81
Frederick the Great, 24

freeze-dried potatoes, 18–19
french fry machine, 89–92, 108
"french-"style food, 28
frozen fries, 31, 33–43
 exports of, 14, 93–97, 104
 research on, 36–40, 42–43
 standards for, 71
fry parlor concept, 97–98
fungus, potato, 23

Garnet Chile potato, 29
Gem Russet potato, 48–49
Generation 7 fries, 44–45
genetic alterations, 29, 30, 47–49
Germon, George, 81
Gilder, George, 34, 38
Goodrich, Chauncey E., 29
Gould, Jay and Hal, 85–86
Greenberg, Jack, 51
grilled potatoes, 63
Groves, Leslie, 41

Halal, 96
hamburgers, 1–3, 5, 7, 31, 36, 52–54, 98
Handwerker, Murray, 86–87
Hayes, Isaac, 52
health spa fries, 69–70
Henry, Prince, 24
Henry VIII, King, 20, 21
Hildebrandt's (Williston Park, New York), 84
Holman's (Portland, Oregon), 83
Holzinger, Steve, 70
Hong Kong, 14, 96
Hospitality Works, 84–85, 102–4
Huffaker, Bruce, 46–47
Hutterites, 94

Idaho potato, 16, 17, 29, 30, 34–36, 39–40, 47–49, 81, 82
Idaho Potato Commission, 23, 64
Ireland, 23, 28

Jack in the Box, 12
Jamison, Bill and Cheryl Alters, 63
Jefferson, Thomas, 26–28
Johnson, Brad A., 4, 34, 81
Jones, Evan, 24
J.R. Simplot Co., 94–97
julienne fries, 8, 29, 70
Junior JoJo's, 8

Kartoffel Krieg (Potato War), 23–24
Kellerman, Jonathan, 6
Kelly, Edward C., 90–92, 108
Kennebec potato, 76

ketchup, 1–2, 3, 5, 72, 77, 82–83, 106
Kharasch, Izzy, 84–85, 102–4
Killeen, Johanne, 81
Kroc, Ray, 2, 26, 33–35, 36, 37–40
Krunchie Wedges, 8
Kukes, Maya, 4–5, 83
Kundin, Joel, 80

Lamb, F. Gilbert, 40
Lamb Water Gun Knife, 40
Lamb Weston, 40, 44–45, 108
lattice cuts, 8
Le Caprice (London), 83–84
Logan, Paul, 38–39
Louis XVI, King, 20, 22
Love, John F., 36
low-fat fries, 7, 44, 108
lumchipamundana, 18
Lunden, Joan, 4

Macy's, 31
Malines, Joseph, 25–26
mandrake, 19
Manhattan Project, 40–41
Mansion on Turtle Creek, The (Dallas), 71–72
Mariani, John, 28
Marie Antoinette, 20, 22
Marvel LLC, 44
mashed potatoes, 13
Maxson Food Systems, 31
mayonnaise, 3, 77, 79, 82–83
McCain, 40
McClard's (Hot Springs, Arkansas), 82–83
McDonald's, 2–3, 26, 72
 Burger King fry challenge, 3, 51–53, 54–58
 cultural impact of, 104
 french fry volume of, 11, 12, 13, 40
 Kroc-Simplot pact and, 33–35, 37–40
 potato-frying research, 36–40, 42–43
McLamore, James W., 52–53, 58, 59
Mega-Crunch Juliennes, 8
Mes, Michel A., 65–66
Micron Technology, 42
middle class, 14, 93, 94
Mirco Technology, 90
mishipansinghan, 18
Mr. Potato Head, 51–52
Moon Lake House (Saratoga Springs, New York), 28–29

Napoleon, 23
Nathan's (New York City), 86–87
Nestlé, 40
New York Fries (Toronto, Canada), 85–86
nightshade, 19

Index

Official French Fries Page, The, 66–67
oils and fats, 25, 26, 31, 44, 61–62, 68, 71, 76, 81, 85, 87
Onassis, Jacqueline Kennedy, 4, 61–62
Ore-Ida, 40, 90
Osler, Kathryn Scott, 94
ovenable fries, 7, 44, 45, 68–69

Parmentier, Antoine Augustin, 20–23
Patent Office, U.S., 91
Pat's King of Steaks (Philadelphia), 77
Peru, 17–19
Peter Luger (New York City), 78
Pitman Frialator, 87
Pizarro, Francisco, 19
pommes de terre, 23, 29
pommes frites, 26
Pommes Frites (New York City), 75, 79
Pont-Neuf fries, 29, 70
potato chips, 28–29
poutine, 86
prefrying, 39, 66, 68, 82
Price, Vincent, 72–73
Primanti's (Pittsburgh), 80

quality control, 48–49
Quechua Indians, 18–19
Ramsden, Harry, 25
Ranger Russet potato, 47
Read, Richard, 93–97
Reichl, Ruth, 7, 78
Rhoades, Richard E., 17, 18–19
Roberts, Nora, 4
Roosevelt, Franklin D., 40
Rough Out Thin Cuts, 8
Rushmore, Steve, 84
Russet Burbank potato, 16, 17, 29, 30, 34–36, 39–40, 47–49, 81, 82

Salaman, Redcliffe N., 23–25
Schlosser, Eric, 108
Schumer, Fran, 7
scoop, french fry, 42–43
Scull, Jonathan, 79
Sehelian, Ray, 4
Seven Years' War, 20–23
Sgubin, Marta, 4, 61–62
Shakespeare, William, 17
shapes
    french fry, 6, 8, 9, 12, 13–14, 29, 45, 65–66, 70, 83–84, 86, 102–4
    potato, 18–19, 29, 30, 60
shoestring fries, 8, 13, 70
shredded fries, 70
Shribman, David, 81

Silva, Livie, 85–86
Simplot, John Richard (Jack), 33–35, 37–40, 42
Simplot (J.R.) Co., 94–97
Singapore, 96
Skincredibles, 8
skin-on fries, 8, 13–14, 45
sleep problems, 4
soufflé cut, 70
South America, 17–19, 20
spa fries, 69–70
Spanish sweet potato, 20
spices, 63, 77
Starbucks, 98
steak fries, 8
stealth fries, 3, 45, 51–53, 54–58
Steingarten, Jeffrey, 72
Stern, Jane and Michael, 77
storability, potato, 31, 39, 47–49, 64
super-sizing, 45
Suzy Q's, 6, 8
sweet potatoes, 20

Taco Bell, 45–46
Taiwan, 14, 104
Tasty Fries Inc., 90–92, 108
Tege, 90
temperature
    for baked french fries, 68
    for french fries, 36–37, 64, 66, 69, 71–72
    for potato storage, 48, 64
Thayer, Chris, 68–69
Thomason, John, 82–83
Toklas, Alice B., 68
toppings, 1–2, 3, 5, 12, 26, 72, 76–77, 79, 82–83, 86, 106, 108
Trager, James, 25
Trillin, Calvin, 4, 86–87
Tudge, Colin, 7
'21' Club (New York City), 5, 7

vending machines, 89–92, 108
Verhofstad, Guy, 65
vinegar, 3, 26, 77, 86

waffle cuts, 8, 13, 45
Watson, James L., 104
Websites, 54–57, 65–67
wedge fries, 8, 13
Weimer, Ralph, 42–43
World War I, 31
World War II, 38–39, 91

Yukon gold potato, 81

Zuckerman, Larry, 19–20, 26, 31

ABOUT THE AUTHOR

DAVID GRAULICH writes a nationally syndicated humor column, performs regular commentaries on National Public Radio, and is most recently the author of *Dial 9 to Get Out!,* a humorous look at office life. An avid and enthusiastic fan of hamburgers, french fries, and hot dogs, he resides with his family in San Bruno, California.